MW01479913

THE ORVIS POCKET GUIDE TO
Fly Fishing
for Steelhead

Books by John Shewey

Fly Fishing for Summer Steelhead
Northwest Fly Fishing, Trout and Beyond
*Fly Fishing Pacific Northwest Waters: Trout &
    Beyond II*
Oregon Blue-Ribbon Fly Fishing Guide
Washington Blue-Ribbon Fly Fishing Guide
Idaho Blue-Ribbon Fly Fishing Guide
On the Fly Guide to the Northwest
Steelhead River Journal: North Umpqua
Wingshooter's Guide to Oregon
*Spey Flies and Dee Flies: Their History and
    Construction*
Mastering the Spring Creeks: A Fly Angler's Guide
*Alpine Angler: A Fly Fisher's Guide to the Western
    Wilderness*

THE ORVIS POCKET GUIDE TO
Fly Fishing for Steelhead

Flies, Gear, and Strategies for Taking Fish in Rivers and Streams

JOHN SHEWEY

Illustrations by Rod Walinchus

THE LYONS PRESS
Guilford, Connecticut
An imprint of The Globe Pequot Press

Copyright © 2003 by John Shewey

Illustrations by Rod Walinchus

ALL RIGHTS RESERVED. No part of this book may be reproduced or transmitted in any form by any means, electronic or mechanical, including photocopying and recording, or by any information storage and retrieval system, except as may be expressly permitted in writing from the publisher. Requests for permission should be addressed to The Lyons Press, Attn: Rights and Permissions Department, P.O. Box 480, Guilford, CT 06437.

The Lyons Press is an imprint of The Globe Pequot Press

10 9 8 7 6 5 4 3 2 1

Printed in Canada

ISBN 1–59228–346–2

Library of Congress Cataloging-in-Publication Data

Shewey, John.
     The Orvis pocket guide to fly fishing for steelhead : flies, gear, and strategies for taking fish in rivers and streams / John Shewey ; illustrations by Rod Walinchus.
          p. cm.
     Includes bibliographical references (p.   ) and index.
     ISBN 1-59228-346-2 (trade cloth)
     1. Steelhead fishing. 2. Fly fishing. I. Title: Fly fishing for steelhead. II. Title. SH687.7.S49 2003
     799.17'57—dc22
                                                            2003024857

CONTENTS

INTRODUCTION

Swift, wild, muscular rivers. Deep wades and long casts. Graceful flies and contemplative anglers cognizant of their sport's rich traditions. For generations, steelhead have captured and captivated the hearts and minds and souls of fly anglers in the Pacific Northwest. These remarkable seagoing salmonids, unique in their life history, reign as North America's greatest gamefish, akin to the Atlantic salmon of the British Isles and eastern Canada.

Taking steelhead on a fly represents one of the ultimate expressions of the artistic nature of our chosen method of fishing. The sport enjoys a rich literary tradition spawned by a remarkable fish that has inspired great anglers and great writers to dedicate their lives to the pursuit of steelhead on the fly.

The steelhead defies our attempts to categorize and understand its behavior, its mysterious nature endearing this fish to us as surely as its propensity for great fight. Unlike its relatives, the five species of Pacific salmon, the steelhead is an individual. Steelhead depart the Pacific as individuals to seek out their natal waters, while salmon arrive in hordes. Their relative scarcity makes them all the more precious. A thousand salmon might occupy a single pool, while a thousand yards of river may harbor but a handful of steelhead.

Despite the mystery surrounding their behavior and the relative scarcity in their ranks, steelhead remain reasonably easy to take on a fly. That doesn't mean you catch lots of them; it simply means that the technique for taking them is decidedly easy to learn and execute. But it requires you to love fishing more than you love catching, because many, many casts go into each hookup. Therein lies the challenge: You must immerse yourself in the steelhead's world, learning to relish everything about a steelhead river and your interaction with it.

You must pursue the steelhead with a great deal of faith and with an equal dose of patience. Accomplished steelhead anglers never waver in their faith; they never consciously consider that patience has anything to do with it, because they simply love the fishing. And when a steelhead occasionally accommodates their efforts, dedicated anglers momentarily gain the pinnacle of a sport that rewards those whose reasons for fishing transcend the catching.

The catching, however, is the motivation, so study the techniques, strategies, and other skills needed to earn your success in bringing steelhead to the fly. But remember that the journey matters; the fishing matters. Go astream in your pursuit of steelhead not only to match wits with one of the world's greatest gamefish, but also to relish the waters in which they swim and the angling friendships these steelhead will help you forge along the way.

STEELHEAD LIFE HISTORY

"Steelhead have been fighting their way up the turbulent rapids and waterfalls of western rivers for centuries but the complete details of their life cycles are still not fully known."

—Enos Bradner, 1950

In many ways, steelhead resemble their anadromous brethren, the five species of Pacific salmon. Like salmon, steelhead spawn in clean, cold rivers from Alaska to California. The juveniles remain in their natal rivers for one to three years and then migrate downstream to the Pacific, where they reap the ocean's bounty. After one to four years in the ocean, steelhead—like salmon—feel the spawning urge and return to their home rivers to begin the cycle again.

After spawning, however, adult steelhead do not perish like Pacific salmon. Once their eggs are fertilized and safely buried in clean gravel, the adults again voyage downstream. Those steelhead that survive their postspawn outmigration (these fish are called kelts) may return to spawn yet again the following year. Generally, the shorter the spawning run, the more likely is a steelhead to survive to spawn again. Short coastal rivers abound with repeat spawners. Biologists in southeast Alaska have documented individual fish spawning as many as five times. Those steelhead that

Spawning summer steelhead. For ethical reasons, anglers must leave them undisturbed, but they are fun to watch!

migrate far inland rarely survive the return trip to the ocean in their spent condition.

Regardless of the length of their spawning runs, steelhead lose so much body mass during their stay in freshwater that those surviving to reach the ocean again spend the ensuing months regaining lost weight. Thus, multiple spawning runs have little bearing on a steelhead's size. Instead, the number of consecutive years spent at sea before the first spawning run dictates size. Steelhead that spend one year at sea typically return as fairly small fish, ranging from two to eight pounds or so depending on their oceanic food supply. On the other hand, those rare "three-salt" and "four-salt" fish reach trophy size.

Also, two distinct races of steelhead exhibit significantly different life histories. Summer-run steelhead—the more popular with fly anglers—enter the river systems between late April and early autumn. The exact timing varies substantially. In northern California, most adult summer steelhead return to the rivers during late spring, before flows diminish and water tem-

The author with a summer-run steelhead taken during hot July weather.

peratures warm beyond their liking. Further north, many summer fish depart the Pacific as late as July.

Sexually undeveloped upon leaving the ocean, these summer-run steelhead require many months in fresh water before they mature and are able to spawn. In some rivers, especially in the southern parts of their range, summer steelhead seek deep, cool pools in which to wait out the summer heat. Autumn brings a respite from the warm water, and spawning occurs during winter, generally in January and February. Most summer steelhead spawn in headwater tributaries that frequently run dry, or at least too low for safe passage during summer and fall. Hence these summer-run fish have adapted the strategy of waiting for winter rains to swell the spawning tributaries. The juvenile steelhead then depart the seasonal streams during spring and head for the safety of year-round flows.

Conversely, winter steelhead arrive in prime, ripe condition, able to reproduce immediately upon reaching the spawning grounds. Typically spawning in the main river and its larger tributaries, winter steelhead enter their natal rivers between December and April. Their range is coastal, and only in a few cases do their spawning runs extend beyond a hundred miles. The long-distance champions among steelhead are the summer fish that travel nine hundred miles from the Pacific to interior Idaho.

The terms "summer steelhead" and "winter steelhead" denote the specific life history of each race as exhibited by the two respective spawning strategies. Anglers, however, often use terms like "fall steelhead" or "spring steelhead." The former denotes late-arriving, summer-run fish, while the latter is often applied to winter steelhead arriving during March and April. Likewise, the phrase "summer steelheading" invariably denotes fishing for summer-run fish, but "winter steelheading" sometimes means fishing for winter-run fish and under other, more suspect circumstances—such as when the fish are spawning—describes fishing for summer-run fish during winter (likewise for the term "spring steelheading").

Within both races of steelhead one finds myriad populations whose specific behaviors and characteristics derive from their particular life histories in their natal watersheds. Specific populations tend to differ in the timing of their runs, the amount of time the fish spend in the river and in the ocean, and in many other attributes.

Several populations of steelhead, for example, exhibit the so-called "half-pounder" life history. Found most prominently in Oregon's Rogue River and California's Klamath River, half-pounders are small, immature steelhead that spend only a few months in the ocean before returning to their natal rivers in the fall. The following spring they again migrate to the ocean, to return later as adult fish.

Oregon and Washington host two taxonomically distinct steelhead subgroups, the coastal steelhead (*Oncorhynchus mykiss irideus*) that ranges from California to Alaska and the inland Columbia Basin steelhead (*Oncorhynchus mykiss gairdneri*), whose long-range migrations reach the far corners of northeastern Oregon, southeastern Washington, and central Idaho.

Steelhead share with Pacific salmon the genus name *Oncorhynchus*. Until fairly recently both steelhead and rainbow trout were classified as *Salmo gairdneri*. The steelhead was generally understood to be a seagoing variety of the rainbow trout. But genetic research proved the taxonomy to be far from settled and indicated that the steelhead—and thus the rainbow trout—are more closely akin to Pacific salmon than to trout. Confusing matters further is the indigenous redband trout of the Great Basin, now called *Oncorhynchus mykiss newberri,* and by definition historically inaccessible to waters draining to the Pacific Ocean.

In any event, though steelhead are now considered more closely related to salmon than to trout, their be-

A summer steelhead beginning to regain the coloring of a rainbow trout.

haviors rarely resemble those of Pacific salmon. By comparison, steelhead behave individually. They do not school as salmon do in the ocean and upon their return to fresh water. Instead, steelhead roam the seas as individuals and return to their natal rivers alone or in small groups. In fresh water, steelhead act far more aggressively than Pacific salmon.

These two characteristics—individualism and aggressiveness—separate steelhead from Pacific salmon and make steelhead the most prized fly rod quarry in the West. Anglers relish steelhead for their relative scarcity in the river compared to the hordes of salmon that invade in huge waves and schools during their spawning runs. Steelhead often prove elusive, but when the persistent angler finds them these remarkable gamefish often chase flies aggressively, endearing themselves to anglers in a way Pacific salmon could never hope to match.

Yet our addiction to steelhead goes beyond the rarity of each unlikely encounter with an aggressive member of their tribe. They make for better sport, especially for the contemplative soul, for the steelhead is not doomed to die upon spawning as is the salmon. For many veteran steelhead fly anglers, the pursuit of salmon in fresh water hardly seems sporting, considering the salmon is on its death march. The steelhead, conversely, allures us in part because it offers sport in season and then goes about its reproductive cycle only to survive the rigors of migration and with luck repeat the cycle yet again the next year.

STEELHEAD PAST AND PRESENT

Historically steelhead ranged from the Santo Domingo River in northern Baja, Mexico to the Cold Bay area on the Alaska Peninsula. Inland steelhead reached deep into the far-flung corners of eastern Washington and eastern Oregon and all the way to the headwaters of the Salmon River in central Idaho. Indeed, Snake River steelhead and salmon once migrated as far as northwestern Nevada.

But the activities of man spelled doom for the steelhead populations on the southern and eastern fringes of this range, and no longer do these seagoing wanderers return to most of the Snake River tributaries nor in any appreciable numbers to southern California.

The culprits in steelhead decline are easily identified, as stated in the California Department of Fish and Game's 1996 Steelhead Restoration and Management Plan: "The major factor causing the decline in California is freshwater habitat loss and degradation. This has resulted mainly from three factors: inadequate stream flows, blocked access to historic spawning and rearing areas due to dams, and human activities that discharge sediment and debris into watercourses."

Throughout their range, steelhead face similar threats, and some populations have been extirpated entirely. But there is good news too. The 1980s ushered in an era of more enlightened watershed management, and while the usual time-tested threats remain problematic in many areas, fisheries managers are increasingly learning to mitigate the damage through new land use policies.

Many rivers remain highly productive spawning grounds for wild steelhead and not surprisingly these tend to be the rivers offering the best preserved or restored habitat. Wild steelhead now enjoy the stewardship of myriad watchdog groups, including Trout Unlimited, The Wild Steelhead Society, CalTrout, The Federation of Fly Fishers, and other organizations. Also, enlightened fisheries managers continue to fight for an end to highly destructive land use practices, such as steep-slope logging along sensitive watercourses.

Meanwhile, wild steelhead stocks continue to be bolstered by hatchery stocks, but increasingly fisheries managers are leaning toward using local genetic stock to raise hatchery steelhead for particular waters. Oregon's North Umpqua River has thus far proven an effective model for this policy. For many years, native

A big, wild summer steelhead.

North Umpqua steelhead, trapped at Rock Creek, have supplied the broodstock for the hatchery-reared summer steelhead planted in the river to supplement the native runs. Superimposing hatchery fish over populations of native fish presents an inarguable danger to the spawning productivity of the wild population, but few would disagree that raising and planting fish from local broodstocks is better than introducing genetic stock originating in other river systems.

During decades past, fisheries managers sometimes used hatchery fish to replace extinct or severely depressed indigenous stocks. In other places, hatchery fish provide steelhead fisheries where none existed historically. The Great Lakes, of course, provide the

A heavy, chrome-bright, winter-run steelhead.

quintessential example of the latter case. Steelhead and Pacific salmon now thrive in the lakes and their tributaries.

Such cases exist in the Northwest as well, including Oregon's McKenzie River and other nearby tributaries to the Willamette River. Historically these rivers hosted a tremendous run of native winter steelhead, but summer steelhead couldn't negotiate the falls at Oregon City during the low-water period of summer. During the middle of the twentieth century, flood control, hydroelectric, and water storage projects included new dam construction on all the Willamette's major tributaries. Later, fish passage facilities were built at Willamette Falls, and in the early 1970s Oregon Department of Fish and Wildlife biologists planted Skamania-strain summer steelhead smolts in the McKenzie and other tributaries.

The project paid huge dividends, creating widespread opportunities for anglers to pursue summer-run steelhead where no such fisheries had ever existed. During its best years, this summer run exceeds thirty thousand fish. In this case, hatchery steelhead were not superimposed over a native population of summer-run fish. Yet biologists remain concerned over the possibility of hatchery-produced summer steelhead diluting the genetic purity of the system's native winter fish. These winter fish—whose migration is among the longest for such steelhead—already suffer the indignity of having at least 80 percent of the their historic spawning grounds blocked by the aforementioned dams.

Winter brings many magical moments to Northwest steelhead waters.

Indeed, genetic dilution ranks as the primary concern in watersheds harboring both native and hatchery-produced steelhead. Studies continue to show that spawning success among wild steelhead decreases as mixing with hatchery fish increases.

Nonetheless, hatcheries remain a significant ingredient in the management of many steelhead sport fisheries throughout most of the fish's range. The plain fact is that many rivers could no longer sustain viable sport fisheries if not for the addition of hatchery-reared fish, so increasingly watershed managers must balance the desire to preserve and enhance native stocks with the need to satisfy the demands of sport anglers.

The dichotomy forms an explosive issue, and one can hardly envy fisheries managers their task of satisfying the demands of sportsmen to provide productive fisheries while still finding ways to protect native stocks. But protect the original stocks we must. As Trey Combs has so aptly pointed out: "On some rivers, such as Washington's Washougal, the native steelhead is now nearly extinct. Wherever it is still possible to do so, these fragile numbers, this irreplaceable gene pool, must be preserved."

2

RODS, REELS, AND LINES

"His fight has the boldness and dash of a cavalry charge. He bounces and tail-walks and explodes into a flashing run. He keeps your heart in your mouth or down in your boots up to his very last gasp. . ."

—Clark C. Van Fleet, 1951

Adult Pacific steelhead typically range from five to more than twenty pounds, depending largely on the specific watershed in which they were spawned. Once hooked, these spectacular gamefish fight hard, running with fast river currents. Some fish jump wildly; others stick doggedly to the depths. They are ideally suited to rods in the 7- to 9-weight range. Having said that, I'll readily admit to having taken lots of steelhead on a 6-weight trout rod, though such tackle is utterly inadequate for really large fish.

So if you own a fairly stout, nine- to ten-foot, 6-weight rod, you are already reasonably equipped to begin your steelhead fly-fishing adventures on waters dominated by fish in single-digit weights. However, if you persist as a steelhead fly angler and certainly if you fish rivers known for double-digit trophies, start shopping for a heavier rod geared specifically to the task of handling big, strong fish.

Steelhead—large, fast, and powerful—require stout tackle.

Steelhead anglers embrace both single-handed rods and two-handed Spey rods. Spey rods range from eleven to sixteen feet in length and are designed for a specific style of roll casting developed long ago on the River Spey in Scotland. Despite misinformed reports of the Spey rod's relative newness to the sport of steelheading, some British Columbia fly anglers were using two-handed rods early in the twentieth century.

Meanwhile, single-handed rods remain the more popular choice among steelhead anglers, even though more and more Spey-casting enthusiasts appear every year on many Northwest rivers. For large rivers—and many of them are very large indeed—choose a rod nine and a half to ten feet long and matched to a 7-, 8-, or 9-weight line. My own preference is a fast or moderately fast ten-foot, 8-weight rod. Long rods excel in lifting lots of line off the water and in keeping it off the water on the backcast when you're wading deep. Significantly, ten-footers are also safer, as they outperform shorter rods at keeping large flies away from your face in breezy conditions.

When choosing a reel for steelhead, look for a model that offers a strong, smooth drag system and also plenty of capacity for line and at least two hundred yards of backing. A steelhead reel must be capable of performing flawlessly in virtually all conditions, from sunny and hot to cold and wet and everything in between. Your reel will get wet, so its drag system

The author prefers a 10-foot, 8-weight rod such as the Orvis Trident TLS.

Steelhead demand reels with good drag systems and capacity for at least 200 yards of 20-pound backing.

must be unaffected by immersion in water. Also, choose a reel free of "line traps," such as handles or drag knobs on which fly line or running line can hang up. I once owned a beautiful and expensive reel whose drag system performed remarkably well, but whose S-curve handle frequently snagged and trapped my line.

Fly lines for steelhead fishing run the gamut from standard floating fly lines to highly specialized line systems. What follows is a discussion of the numerous options, and while line systems can get complicated, remember that you can simplify steelhead fly angling to the point of owning a floating fly line for summer steelhead and a high-density sink-tip fly line for winter steelhead.

TWO-HANDED RODS

Two-handed rods, often called Spey rods, have gained widespread popularity on the West Coast. For many anglers, the long rods allow for increased line control on the water and thus increased fly control. Indeed, controlling the speed and depth of the fly rank among the most significant tactical factors in hooking steelhead. For reasonably practiced Spey casters, the long rods also allow for easy distance casting, which comes into play on large waters like Washington's Skagit River, Idaho's Clearwater River, or British Columbia's Thompson River.

Don't, however, make the switch to the two-handed rod as a substitute for distance casting. Experienced steelhead anglers should possess the ability to cast all the line they need with a single-handed rod. It's all a matter of practice. I did just enough guiding to cure myself of it, and while I lasted I was always amazed that dedicated fly anglers would practice their golf strokes three days a week, but never practice casting.

The two-handed rod excels on water devoid of backcasting room or water where the extra length of the rod allows you to fish midriver slots at a steeper angle of presentation (see chapters 4–6). Often touted for their abilities on big water, the Spey rods also work wonders on small rivers, where they allow the angler to use the rod tip to work the fly slowly across the flow even when casting more across stream than down.

In addition, the two-handed rods excel in windy conditions, especially on large rivers. A strong wind can make life miserable for steelheaders armed with single-handed rods, but practiced Spey casters can battle such conditions effectively with the long rods. And two-handed rods are better suited to casting really large flies, such as the No. 3/0 and 4/0 monstrosities used to good advantage for giant steelhead on British Columbia's Skeena system and elsewhere.

The two-handed rods certainly suffer a few drawbacks. For starters, they are cumbersome in all respects except during the actual casting. A fifteen-foot rod is a lot of tackle to haul over brushy riverside trails. Also, landing fish, especially large fish, requires a beach of some kind or the aid of a fishing partner. I once watched a Spey caster battle a thirty-inch fish on the North Umpqua, a river that flows through a steep, bedrock canyon and which offers few good beaches for landing fish.

The angler had hooked the fish from the top of a large rock protruding from chest-deep water and played the steelhead perhaps a little too long. Departing his casting station atop the boulder, the angler waded across a narrow channel to a steep, riprap bank cluttered with willows and other brush. Here the battle, which would by now have been over with a single-handed rod, took on increasing difficulties as the angler struggled to negotiate the rod tip through branches and brush while the ten-pound steelhead continually struggled to free itself.

Feeling sorry for this spirited steelhead, I scrambled down the steep bank and offered my assistance to the angler. He welcomed my help, so I negotiated the brush and boulders to make my way down the bank, where I tailed his fish. Gently we revived the native buck until, with a flick of its broad tail, the fish disappeared into the North Umpqua's emerald depths. The angler proved rather inexperienced, and his struggles at landing the fish with the long rod hardly dented his enthusiasm for hooking his first North Umpqua steelhead. I didn't dare dampen his spirits on such a momentous occasion, so I kept my opinions to myself. With luck he realized in retrospect that this particular pool was no place for a Spey caster fishing alone, for had I not been there to rescue the poor fish, he may well have been played out to fatal exhaustion while the angler struggled with the terrain.

So each style of casting, with its accompanying tackle, enjoys its advantages and suffers its disadvantages. Usually the choice simply boils down to personal preference. Some anglers prefer the methodical rhythm of the Spey cast; others enjoy the sharp, brutal precision of a double-hauled cast with the single-handed rod. Pick your poison and then concentrate on the more important aspects of steelheading: reading and covering the water.

LINE SYSTEMS

Today's steelhead angler benefits from a vast array of well-made specialty lines designed to meet virtually any conceivable fishing situation. Recent innovations include multi-tip fly lines with interchangeable tip sections of varying sink rates. These are especially convenient for winter steelhead angling, where anglers must fish the fly deeper in the water column than is required for summer-run steelhead. Line manufacturers make these multi-tip lines to fit both single-handed rods and Spey rods.

Fly fishing for summer steelhead ranks as the simplest form of the sport, in that you rarely need anything but a floating line. Owing to their aggressive nature and to ideal water temperatures, summer steelhead tend to chase flies for considerable distances, enamoring themselves to us for their willingness to rise toward the surface to take wet flies and dry flies fished on floating lines. So the ideal line for most summer steelheading situations is a weight-forward floating line. The designation on the packaging will read WF8F, which means "weight-forward, 8-weight, floating" fly line. Of course you should match the specific line weight to your 7-, 8-, or 9-weight rod.

While the weight-forward line is the most useful for steelhead angling, double-taper floating lines might be better suited to certain circumstances. Double-taper lines feature a long, level "belly" section with identical tapers on both ends. They excel at roll casting, making them popular on small rivers with little backcasting room.

Sometimes anglers opt for sink-tip or intermediate fly lines for summer fishing, especially early and late in the season or at midday, when there is intense sunlight on the water. Standard ten-foot sink-tips are quite popular, although sink-tip lines come in a variety of tip lengths. Sink-tip lines are generally designated something like WF8F/S, with a further designation describing the length and sink rate, or density, of the sinking section.

During the winter season, fly anglers confront more challenging water conditions and steelhead less prone to chase flies aggressively. It is then more important to fish the fly somewhat deeper in the flow and closer to the fish. You can achieve and maintain depth by using varying densities and styles of sinking fly lines, by fishing with weighted flies, or by doing both. Flexibility pays dividends during the winter, so most anglers match their tackle to specific water conditions.

Multi-tip fly lines allow such versatility, as do shooting-taper systems, which we'll discuss momentarily. The multi-tip lines are packaged as a set of sink-tip sections, each with a different density and therefore a different sink rate. These tips, usually twenty feet or more in length, include a loop at one end so they can easily be attached to another loop at the end of the running line, which is a length of small-diameter, floating fly line. The result is basically the same as a sink-tip, weight-forward fly line, but in this case you choose the sink rate of the tip portion and match that sink rate to the water conditions.

Another option for winter steelheading is to choose water that matches your tackle rather than choosing tackle to confront whatever water characteristics you encounter. In other words, if you enjoy fishing boulder-strewn pocket water where a high-density sinking line would simply hang up in the rocks, then choose a floating line/long leader/weighted fly combination. Conversely, if you prefer classic "swing water," characterized by a cobble or gravel streambed, opt for the sinking or sink-tip line systems.

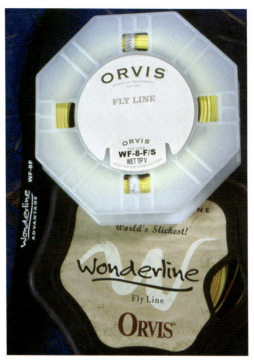

Year-round steelhead anglers need both floating and sink-tip lines.

Either approach is equally acceptable. Some winter steelhead anglers enjoy the dynamic challenge of continually mastering new water types. They embrace a wide array of strategies and tactics, always matching their tackle and technique to the water they encounter. Other steelheaders prefer the opposite approach: They become enamored with the intricacies of one particular method and seek water conducive to their chosen strategy. These days, for example, I prefer to pursue winter steelhead exclusively on waters where I can swing fanciful, unweighted flies with little danger of losing tackle to the rocks.

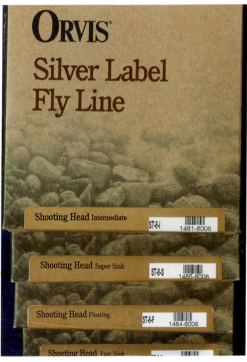

Year-round steelhead anglers need both floating and sink-tip lines.

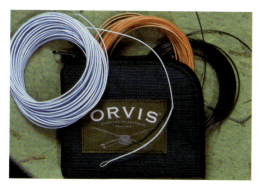

Many anglers prefer shooting taper systems with interchangeable heads ranging in density from floating to fast-sinking.

SHOOTING TAPER SYSTEMS

A shooting taper or "shooting head" system consists of a short (typically thirty to forty feet) length of fly line attached to a small-diameter running line. Conceptually, a shooting taper system is similar to a weight-forward fly line: The idea is to place most of the line's density in the front section and then "shoot" the line on the forward cast to achieve distance. In design, the shooting head differs from the weight-forward fly line in its multi-piece construction and usually in the smaller diameter of the running line. The multi-tipped fly lines described above are closely akin to a shooting taper system, except that they usually come with floating fly line as the running line.

In the hands of a reasonably practiced caster, the shooting taper system is a more efficient version of the weight-forward fly line. The fly line, no matter how slick its coating, causes more friction in the rod guides than does the monofilament or similar materials used in running lines. Thus from a pure casting standpoint, running lines shoot through the guides better than a fly line, no matter how radical the weight-forward design. A shooting taper system using monofilament running line casts effortlessly. With practice, moderately skilled casters can easily throw shooting heads eighty or ninety feet with a single backcast.

Does that make a shooting head a better choice for steelhead fishing? Not necessarily. They suffer certain drawbacks. First, a shooting taper system is virtually impossible to mend once it's on the water because the thin running line does not possess enough weight. Second, the head system proves rather inefficient in short-line situations. It excels at distance casting, for which it is designed, but a standard double-taper or weight-forward fly line is far better suited to rivers where the average cast rarely exceeds sixty feet.

So, full fly lines are a better choice anytime mending is important, such as when you fish waters with complex current structures, or where your casting station leaves you at a positional disadvantage that can be remedied only by repositioning, or mending, the fly line once it is on the water. Likewise, full fly lines work best in roll-casting situations where the bank leaves no room for any kind of backcast. However, the shooting taper system often outperforms full fly lines in areas of *limited* backcast room, because with most shooting heads you need only enough room behind you for forty to fifty feet of line to make a forward cast of twice that distance.

Generally, shooting taper systems perform best on large rivers where long-distance casting offers some advantage. On such waters, the head system effectively speeds up your fishing because you need only one or two backstrokes to generate each maximum-distance cast. In this sense, anglers who learn to minimize their false casting with regular weight-forward fly lines gain the advantage of covering more water in the course of a day's fishing.

During the summer season, floating and intermediate heads are most useful. They are also easier to cast and manage than sinking heads. In fact, you should learn to cast a floating or intermediate shooting taper before attempting the more challenging sinking heads.

All the major line manufacturers now offer shooting taper lines in a wide array of sink rates and matched to specific rod weights. The designation usually reads something like ST8F (for an 8-weight, floating, shooting taper) or ST9S for a 9-weight sinking head, in which case another designation will follow indicating the sink rate or density of the line. Next you'll need running line, which can range from small-diameter fly line to various monofilaments. Stretch the running line by hand after stripping it off

Two-handed Spey-casting rods are popular on Northwest rivers.

the reel. So stretched, it will remain coil–less until re-wound and stored on the reel for a time. I've long forgotten who authored the idea, but I once read that the best way to stretch the running line is to hook a strong steelhead and let the fish do it for you—I'll go along with that!

CASTING TIPS

Through all my years working in fly shops, guiding, and teaching I've noticed that the inability to cast for distance is the single most prevalent and curable problem adversely affecting most fly anglers. Even experienced anglers often benefit markedly from a few basic pointers, and in steelhead angling (not to mention saltwater fishing and many other venues), distance casting comes in terribly handy.

Casting for distance is synonymous with casting with efficiency: The better your casting stroke, the easier you generate distance. The key is to learn to form tight, wedge-shaped loops, and this is accomplished only by perfecting your stroke. Nothing beats hands-on instruction, so if you need lessons, by all means go get them—find a qualified casting instructor and learn the basics. Then practice and practice often.

The Federation of Fly Fishers uses a casting instructor certification process in an effort to help elevate the standards of instruction. However, plenty of great casting instructors come with no certification of any kind.

On large steelhead rivers, distance-casting skills come in handy.

The author casts over a broad pool.

My longtime fishing partner is hands down the best casting instructor I've ever known, and he's never been trained or certified in any way. He simply combines a highly practiced mastery of fly casting with uncommon patience and a rare ability to effectively convey the principles of fly casting in an easily understood manner.

In any case, I've included here a few tips on casting based on what I see as fairly common mistakes or oversights. Regardless whether you fish a standard fly line or some form of shooting taper system, these techniques can aid in improving your distance and casting efficiency.

LOOP FORMATION

The term "loop" is used to describe the shape and dimensions of your fly line as it unfurls toward its target on the forward cast or as it begins to straighten behind you on the backcast. The size and shape of your casting loop determines the distance and direction the line will travel and is itself determined by the characteristics of your casting stroke, or the precise manner in which you cast the fly rod. Essentially, the smaller and tighter the loop the more efficient the cast, and the more efficient the cast the more effortlessly you achieve distance and precision.

The ideal loop is wedge-shaped rather than round at its leading edge, and the upper and lower portions of the line are close together and nearly parallel. Obviously the loop is highly dynamic, but its characteristics are easily studied, especially by an observer standing

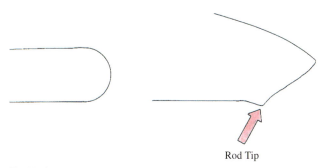

Rod Tip

The ideal loop is wedge-shaped on its leading edge, rather than round.

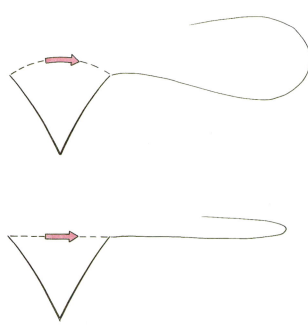

The rod tip should trace a straight path, rather than an arc, during the cast.

off to one side. A wedge-shaped loop is what we call a "tight loop" and is characteristic of an efficient distance cast. The round loop, while efficient to a point, often signifies a slight arc in the path of the rod tip, and an arcing movement robs the cast of power.

Sometimes termed a "power stroke," the distance cast differs markedly from the casting stroke used to generate modest distances in trout or warmwater fishing. While the typical cast relies on a rather short rod stroke, the distance cast requires a long rod stroke. In the old days, we learned to cast by envisioning the numbers on a clock: The perfect cast relied on a rod stroke that traveled from 10 o'clock to 2 o'clock and back to 10 o'clock. On a short cast, especially with modern graphite rods, even 11 o'clock to 1 o'clock might prove ideal. In other words, the rod stops at those two points on the clock. The clock idea has lost favor with casting instructors these days, but I find it a fine way to visualize the *angle* of the rod at the terminal ends of the casting stroke, though not the *path* that the rod tip travels.

Whereas a typical short cast would stop at 10 o'clock in front and 2 o'clock in the rear, the rod must travel further on the backstroke for a distance cast. You will still stop the rod close to 2 o'clock, giving the backstroke its power generated by the rod flex, but instantaneously thereafter you will allow your arm to drift rearward and the rod angle to flatten slightly behind you. (See diagram on page 36.) On the ensuing forward stroke, you generate additional impetus through your ability to bend the rod more forcefully because of the extended backstroke. Imagine throwing a baseball: You can toss the ball twenty feet with a flip of the wrist, starting no further back than your ear. But throwing it forcefully across the outfield requires you to cock your arm well behind your head.

So learn to lengthen your rod stroke. Practice often. Remember, a short stroke is ideally suited to shorter casts, but a longer stroke helps with distance casts. The

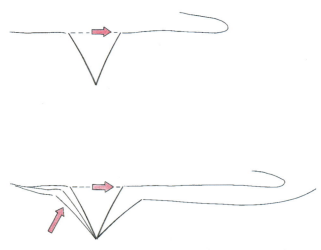

The distance stroke relies on the idea of "rod drift" to help cock the arm and rod for additional impetus on the forward stroke.

basics are simple: The "distance stroke" requires that your casting arm drift rearward during the backcast and that your rod approach parallel to the ground on the backstroke, all the while maintaining the smooth acceleration that defines a good cast. The ensuing forward stroke must then be aimed slightly upward, with a high rod stop in front: The idea is to cast *out over* the water, not *down into* it.

CASTING FAULTS

One common fault of otherwise good casters is to alter the plane in which the backstroke or forward stroke travels. Each stroke must travel along a single plane for maximum efficiency. If the rod curves to the left or right during the forward stroke or backstroke, the cast loses impetus, reducing your ability to throw a tight loop. A curved casting plane saps the rod's "loading" ability. If the backstroke curves, you loose impetus on the forward stroke; if the forward stroke curves, you lose the ability to shoot line effectively as described below, and thus you lose distance on the cast.

Often it's hard to tell that you are curving your casting strokes. The telltale sign on the forward stroke is a cast that curves inward (rarely outward), or to the left for a right-handed caster. A curved backstroke is best detected by having a friend stand directly in line with your cast, just beyond the range of your fly line, and watch the path on which the rod travels. Turning your head to watch your own backstroke often *causes* a curved backstroke. If you want to watch your own backcast, turn your head to the side but don't turn your shoulders. If you find a curve in your stroke, even a minor one, get rid of it—practice making smooth, straight strokes in both directions. Individually you can make the backstroke and forward cast on two different planes, but don't alter the plane one or the other travels along.

Similarly, the rod tip should travel in a straight path from front to back and not in an arc. Even if the rod travels in one plane as required for efficient casting, a rod tip that traces an arcing path from back to front robs the cast of power. An arcing rod tip is revealed by

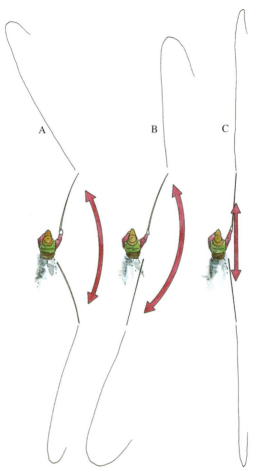

Curved casting strokes rob the cast of power. Viewed from above, A and B are examples of curved strokes. The efficient casting stroke travels in a single plane, as in C.

an open, round loop. Remove the arc and you close the loop, making the casting stroke more efficient. (See diagram.)

Another common hindrance to distance casting is caused by trying to hold too much line in the air during the cast. A long-distance cast relies on the concept of shooting line: You hold line in reserve while making the false cast and then release this line at the end of the forward stroke, causing it to shoot through the guides and out over the water. By effectively shooting line, you can easily make an eighty-foot cast while false-casting just forty or fifty feet of line. False-casting all eighty feet of that fly line usually proves an exercise in utter frustration.

SHOOTING LINE

Shooting line simply means that you release most of the line from your free hand after making the forward cast, rather than trying to hold lots of line in the air during the cast. Weight-forward lines and shooting tapers are designed to take advantage of this idea. Shooting line requires some understanding of what we call "overhang," referring to the amount of the thin-diameter portion of the line extending outside the tip-top guide during the cast. Each line/rod/caster combination has an ideal amount of overhang, which might range from two or three feet with a shooting taper system to fifteen or more feet with a weight-forward fly line. In either case, the overhang is measured from the rear-end taper on the fly line or, in the case of shooting tapers and multi-tips, from the junction between the fly line and the running line.

Shooting line, like all aspects of fly casting, relies on timing as well as technique. To understand the basic idea, first find the junction in your weight-forward line where the thick front taper meets the thin running line. Pull all of the thick portion of the fly line and three feet of the running line beyond the tip-top guide on your rod, with no additional slack line protruding from the reel. Lay this amount of line out in a straight line on the grass. Pick up the line with a single, smooth power stroke as described above, and make a forward cast aimed out *over* the grass, not down *toward* the grass. If you've made a proper cast, you'll feel the line suddenly tug at the reel as the forward cast straightens in front of you. Your powerful cast is begging for more line.

Now strip off about ten feet of line from the reel. Pin this line under the leading finger on your rod hand so the extra line is now forming a narrow loop between the reel and your finger and hanging down to the ground at your side. Make an identical cast, but this time, just as the forward cast straightens over the grass, release your finger from the line and watch it sail out through the rod guides, being pulled along by the forward portion of the fly line. Once you have the timing right, try holding the extra length of line in your off hand, and release it as before upon the completion of the forward stroke.

As you learn to shoot more and more line for long-distance casts, the only issue left facing you is what to do with the line held in reserve as you cast while standing waist deep in a wide river. Most anglers hold the line in two or three large loops, because stripping baskets are completely impractical on swift steelhead rivers. At the completion of each swing, with the line hooked under the index finger on your rod hand, make three long strips of line. These three long strips comprise enough line for one loop. Holding the loop in your left hand after the third strip, make another three strips. Then make the next cast, releasing both loops as you shoot the line.

You can hold three loops in your left hand, but doing so increases the risk of tangling. You can hold two larger loops, but if these longer loops trail too far downstream, they create substantial drag, robbing the cast of its power. One common solution is to hold the first loop in your lips and the next two loops in your left hand as described above.

THE DOUBLE HAUL

The double haul is the principal method for generating additional line speed and thus momentum during the casting stroke. You perform the double haul by using your line hand to make two quick, short pulls (or "hauls") on the line below the first guide. The first haul occurs on the backstroke and the second on the forward stroke. That sounds simple enough, perhaps, but the critically important mechanics and timing of the double haul cannot be learned by reading. You must learn the technique first by watching and then by hands-on practice. Seek out a qualified casting instructor and ask specifically that the double haul be included in the lessons, or watch a casting video that focuses on the technique.

THE WATER HAUL

The water haul is a technique that allows you to load, or bend, the rod without false casting. It works especially well with floating and intermediate lines but can also, with practice, be used with sinking heads and sink-tip lines. Strip in line until you are left with an easily castable length, your intention being to shoot line on the forward stroke to make a long cast. Now pick up that shortened length of line with a single smooth backstroke and then, with the ensuing forward stroke, lay it back on the water in a straight line. Immediately pluck the line off the water and make the fishing cast. The tension from the water provides the impetus normally created by false casting, loading the rod for the forward stroke. Naturally the water haul requires practice, but its mastery markedly improves your efficiency at casting and thus fishing.

LEADERS AND TIPPETS

I have watched skittish steelhead bolt from the pool at the sight and sound of a fly line crashing down on the still surface, and I have seen them scurry away or simply move aside at the sight of a drifting or swinging fly. Yet I cannot honestly attest to having seen leader-shy steelhead, and to prove such behavior occurs I'd need to first rule out those latter two events. So I never undergun the strength of my leader and habitually fish ten- and twelve-pound-test tippets.

Leaders in the eight- to ten-foot range are perfectly suited to dry-line fishing during the summer season and to fishing floating lines with weighted flies during the winter runs. Make sure the leader carries enough butt diameter (at least .023 inch) and rigidity to turn over large flies if you fish patterns larger than No. 6.

When fishing sinking lines or sink-tips, shorten the leader substantially so as not to defeat the purpose of the high-density line. During winter, when I fish 300- and 400-grain sinking heads, I shrink the leader down to a scant three feet in total, including the tippet. Even for heavy-bodied winter steelhead, I rarely if ever use tippets heavier than twelve-pound test. If I happen to hang the fly on some unseen rock, I would certainly rather break off the fly at the tippet than risk losing an entire fly line.

The new fluorocarbon (also called PVDF, or polyvinylidene fluoride) leaders and tippets serve faithfully in steelhead angling. Fluorocarbon is capable of withstanding substantial abuse without weakening, including exposure to sunlight, and is more abrasion resistant than traditional monofilament. Though this is not too significant in western steelhead angling, fluorocarbon also practically disappears underwater, because its index of refraction is close to that of the water. Even with fluorocarbon, always retie your tippet-to-fly knot after each hookup, and periodically check all the knots in the leader system.

The Perfection Loop makes a good fly-to-tippet connection.

The Figure-8 Loop Knot.

For knotting fly to tippet, I prefer the Figure-8 Loop Knot used like a Turle Knot. This simple knot retains virtually all of the original line strength and has never failed me on a hookup with a steelhead. The Figure-8 Loop, used as a Turle, eliminates any free play in the fly, a characteristic considered critical to success by some anglers who espouse fishing the fly on open loop knots. Yet as nearly as I can determine, the lack of free play in my swinging fly has resulted in no deficit whatsoever in my catch rates over the years.

For large flies, you can't beat the Figure-8 Loop, "turled" around the eye of the hook.

Tying the Figure-8 Loop Knot as a Turle.

3

STEELHEAD FLIES

"We sought an answer to the often-heard question: Why does a steelhead take a fly? There is no provable answer."

—Syl MacDowell, 1948

Despite their close kinship to indigenous races of trout, steelhead rarely behave like trout. Only in rare circumstances do they feed for sustenance upon their return to their natal rivers. Such feeding is generally limited to races of small, summer-run steelhead such as those found in Oregon's Rogue River and California's Klamath River. These immature steelhead, which rarely exceed twenty inches in length, feed with increasing frequency the longer they remain in the rivers.

Otherwise, steelhead feeding behavior seems largely unrelated to actual sustenance. After all, a steelhead of eight, ten, or fifteen pounds, having attained such size preying on the ocean's bounty, could hardly sustain itself by feeding on insects in comparatively infertile rivers. So, for the most part, steelhead don't really feed themselves like trout. Sometimes they ingest food items, but certainly not in quantities to suggest that they are feeding for sustenance. Steelhead also ingest inanimate, nonfood items—perhaps as often as they eat real foods.

So why do they take flies? That question has haunted and/or fascinated several generations of Pacific Coast anglers, and the answer remains entirely elusive. Theories abound. Some cite aggressiveness during spawning cycles; others suggest latent feeding instincts revived by the fly. Actually, the sheer quantity of theories testifies to the assertion that pattern choice doesn't matter to the fish.

One certainty is that steelhead are prone to rise for just about anything as often as they are prone to rise for nothing at all. They seem, after all, equally likely to chase a somber little hairwing fly as a bejeweled salmon fly: A small pool on Washington's Grande Ronde once rewarded me with two beautiful wild steelhead, back-to-back, the first on a No. 3/0 Jock Scott and the second on a No. 4 Skunk.

So we must approach our choice of flies with an understanding that particular pattern choice matters little, if at all, to steelhead. Trout anglers, accustomed to matching hatches and being rewarded for their ability to do so effectively, may find the steelhead's behavior rather disconcerting. Conversely, steelhead veterans embrace the inconsistent behaviors of these fish as an invitation to offer them a wide array of different flies.

As trite as this may sound, the most effective fly for steelhead is the one on your leader. Choose a favorite—or perhaps several favorites—and stick with them. The key is to present that fly, no matter the pattern, to as many steelhead as possible in your quest to find an aggressive fish, or a so-called "biter."

DOES THE FLY REALLY MATTER?

Few would dispute the notion that steelhead behave remarkably like Atlantic salmon with regard to their occasional affections toward our flies. And as with Atlantic salmon, we have no idea why steelhead chase and take flies in the first place. The subject of whether the fly pattern matters to the fish incited lively arguments among British Atlantic salmon anglers during the nineteenth century, some of whom insisted that a single fiber or feather or precise shade of color could spell the difference between a fly's success and failure. The same arguments ensue today among steelheaders.

Simple empiricism offers ample evidence of the insignificance of pattern choice: Countless steelhead dressings have proven their effectiveness over the years, and yet no single dressing, color scheme, or style can claim supremacy. Given the centuries-old evolution of the many hundreds of different salmon and steelhead patterns, I should think that if one particular style or color or pattern were indeed more effective than all others, we would all be using that fly by now. Instead, the opposite has occurred: We have more steelhead patterns than ever before and the vast selection continues to expand.

Meanwhile, a steelhead's selectivity to pattern or color or style cannot hope to be tested under the scrutiny of scientific method—too many variables are left unaccounted for no matter what test we might dream up. Still, one summer, mostly just to entertain myself, I engaged in the only test I can devise that comes even remotely close to being scientific.

I fished two flies at a time, close together on the leader, and switched the order of these two flies after each hookup. The idea was to offer a choice to the fish. By changing the lead fly after each hookup I hoped to control the variable of whether a fish chases the first fly regardless of pattern. I fished the flies close enough together to give me reasonable confidence that the fish could study both offerings and choose one or the other.

I stuck with the experiment for an unscientifically short period of time because I soon tired of casting two flies. Nonetheless, I hung in there long enough for my two-fly rig to account for fourteen fish: Six ate the purple fly and four ate the yellow fly. Four fish came unpinned before I could determine which fly was responsible. In seven cases the lead fly was taken, fished just fourteen inches ahead of the dropper fly, which was taken three times.

Scientific? Hardly, but it's a start. A reasonably scientific version of that experiment would include enough hours of fishing to achieve a high number of hookups, flies I like, and trying to fish them in the right places and in the correct manner.

This idea that fly choice just doesn't matter to the fish is a concept that proves rather unpalatable to many novice steelhead anglers and even to many veterans. So they look for a magic bullet—some fly pattern, fly design, or theory thereof that will give them an edge, when in fact such energies would be better spent on learning where and when to find fish and on how best to present the fly.

Over the years, countless anglers have espoused the idea that a single attribute, such as a sniff of bright color or a particular style of hackle feather, somehow elevates an otherwise average fly to some supposed rank among the elite steelhead catchers. On rare occasions these flies gain a widespread following and earn long-standing repute. The classic example is the superbly popular Green-Butt Skunk. The Skunk pattern in all its simplicity has been in general use for half a century. It was devised by one or both of two different people on two different rivers hundreds of miles apart.

Then along came Dan Callaghan, the Oregon-based angler and photographer who has produced some of steelheading's most beautiful photographic images. Callaghan added a butt of fluorescent green to the Skunk and hence was born the Green-Butt Skunk. By the 1980s, the Green-Butt Skunk had become perhaps the single most popular steelhead pattern in the Pacific Northwest, and over the past few decades it has probably accounted for more steelhead than any other single dressing.

Thus arrives a twist on the old chicken-versus-egg argument: Does the Green-Butt Skunk catch more steelhead because it is somehow inherently superior to other patterns, or does it account for more fish because it is fished more than any other fly? Logic, along with long experience, suggests the latter to me. Significantly, if you, unlike me, do in fact believe that the green butt on the Skunk pattern makes all the difference, then you had darn well better stick with that fly. Confidence, after all, counts considerably when angling for a fish that often demands hundreds of casts for each hookup.

WHEN TO CHANGE FLIES

Certainly there are seemingly logical reasons to change flies. Perhaps on a second pass through the same water one might want to offer the fish something new. Or perhaps it makes sense to fish something different than the anglers fishing ahead of you. Or a change in fly might seem appropriate after a fish chases the initial offering without taking it.

Logic, however, rarely applies to steelhead behavior and in each of these scenarios the angler might very well expect identical results—or lack thereof—should no change of fly be made.

Indeed, no less an authority than Sir Herbert Maxwell, the venerable early-twentieth-century British author, relates: "I have killed salmon with the fly in thirty-one different rivers in England, Scotland, Ireland, and Norway, and have never been able to detect preference on the part of the fish for any particular colour or shade of light and dark.

"Fishing just above high tide mark in the Water of Luce," continues Maxwell, "I raised a small fish five times without touching him, changed the fly every time and killed him, seven pounds, at the sixth rise. I cannot think that the result would have been any different had I made no change, which is the course I should follow now in the unromantic light of experience."

The most significant reason to change flies is to change the specific behavior or function of the fly in terms of your tactics. Perhaps, for example, you decide to switch from a waking fly to a wet fly or from a light-wire hook to a heavier offering. These decisions may well effect a change in your success in specific circumstances. Perhaps a fish chases the waking fly but proves too shy to take. Sometimes a wet fly fished on a follow-up presentation does the job. Or maybe a bright sun dictates a larger, heavier fly that shows up better under the midday glare and fishes a little deeper.

I'm a big-fly advocate anyway, but certain circumstances might demand smaller offerings. Some fish become skittish during the skinny-water periods of late summer, often bolting at the splash from a fly line or large fly. This is especially true in shallow, glassy tail-outs and pools found on super-clear streams like Oregon's North Umpqua or Washington's Kalama.

Under such conditions, a conservative approach may pay dividends. Try a small fly to minimize entry splash, and lengthen the leader to reduce line splash. Meanwhile, even under low water conditions, I don't worry over the old advice about drab flies for skittish fish, especially since color seems inconsequential anyway. Nor do I concern myself with such nonsensical wisdom as "dark day, dark fly; bright day, bright fly" or any of its derivations: For me, such theories evaporated long ago in the face of contrary evidence. In other words, I've hooked too many bright-day fish on dark flies and too many dark-day fish on bright flies.

Indeed, fly color seems more attuned to the whims of fashion than to any particular preference of the fish. Each color has enjoyed its moments in the sun during the past hundred years or so, and personally I've yet to find a color that the fish deem inappropriate. Certain rivers gain reputations for being especially suited to particular colors, but this phenomenon seems more a mathematical equation than a preference by the steelhead.

My local river, for example, enjoys a reputation for being especially kind to purple flies. The most popular locally devised patterns are purple, and they probably account for a majority of fish hooked each summer. But they are also used more than flies of any other color. Personally, during the typical season, I hook perhaps 80 percent of my summer fish on two patterns, the Spawning Purple and Forrest Maxwell's Purple Matuka. If I kept track, I'm pretty certain that I'd discover that I fish those two flies about 80 percent of the time.

One summer I broke my own pattern and decided to change flies after every hookup. I never found a fly that wouldn't take a fish, the steelhead in my home rivers apparently being substantially less particular about flies than many anglers pursuing them.

Far from concerning myself with their unpredictable natures, I take the peculiarities of these fish to heart and treat their inexplicable behaviors as an invitation to dress my flies for reasons other than what I think

53

might attract their attention. Instead, I dress the flies that appeal to me. Then I fish with purpose, striving always to improve in the areas that matter far more than fly choice, these being the conjoined arts of presenting the fly in the right way in the right place.

Remember that in this debate we are concerned only with the game of raising a steelhead to a swinging fly. The entire argument might prove devoid of substance when applied to the myriad other methods used by modern steelheaders wherein flies—and lures generously termed "flies"—are fished deep in the flow, often on a dead drift. The specifics of those methods and their application to this debate I will leave to others.

BELIEVE IN YOUR FLY

Anglers who preach particular theories about the supremacy of one fly or style of fly tend to abandon those beliefs over the course of many seasons spent chasing steelhead. In the interim, do their theories, if well publicized, do a disservice to the newcomer? Likely not, for in the case of trout angling, fly choice often proves critical to success. So trout anglers new to steelheading might approach this game with more confidence when armed with some theory that seems to make sense of steelhead and their behavior toward flies.

I've watched this scenario at work: As his casting hours mount in search of that first steelhead, the novice quite logically begins to question his choice in tactics and flies. Along comes some sage who says this fly or that proves predominantly effective under some particular set of circumstances. The novice grabs hold of this new theory, ties or acquires the recommended flies, and then begins angling again with renewed confidence.

And therein lies the key. The confident angler pays attention to detail. She fishes each cast from top to bottom, each pool from head to lip. Eventually her fly dances past a willing combatant, and she hooks that first magnificent steelhead. Along the way, the newcomer learns to enjoy the wading, to appreciate the river and its surroundings, to revel in each well-executed cast.

I watched Jennifer progress rapidly as a steelheader because her primary concern was to enjoy her time on the river, to immerse herself in the beauty and potential of each shimmering pool and each gliding run. Each day astream she marveled at the intricate dance of life playing itself out along the cold, clean flows—the hummingbirds forgoing nectar and buzzing out over the river to catch insects, the families of mergansers and harlequin ducks routinely speeding up-river on powerful wings, the swarming mayflies and caddisflies accompanying the gathering dusk each summer eve.

She fished each run to the best of her ability. Where more experienced casters delivered ninety-foot casts, Jen enjoyed the elation of perfecting each forty-foot stroke. In short, she appreciated the river, its surroundings, and the opportunity to cast across its magical flows. She simply enjoyed the fishing with little concern over the actual catching, and the steelhead rewarded her enthusiasm for playing the game right: Not too many days into her first summer season, Jen hooked two fish in two pools. The first steelhead pounced on the fly and shot out of the river like a rocket, landing with a thunderous "clap." A huge buck of perhaps fourteen or fifteen pounds, the fish threw the hook. Jen was awestruck but hardly disappointed in the outcome, and thirty minutes later she was fast to an eight-pound hen. She played the spirited fish masterfully, and we watched the chrome-bright beauty glide back into the flow just as darkness crept over the summer sky.

Jennifer never questioned her tackle. For what it's worth, her successful fly that evening was a No. 4 Max Canyon, dressed with jungle cock at the shoulders. Despite a complete lack of results on previous evenings that summer, the idea of questioning the fly choice never occurred to her. She bought completely into my theory: Choose a fly that looks good to you and stick with it. Then keep that fly in the water and believe in every cast and every pool.

Of course I had chosen the pattern for Jennifer, but she never questioned the choice because she liked the looks of the fly. Indeed, each angler must ultimately arrive at his or her confidence flies— those particular patterns he or she fishes without questioning the choice. In that sense, pattern choice becomes paramount, for the angler who trusts completely in his or her choice of flies immediately abandons all concerns over whether this or that fly is the better option. Having abandoned such concerns, the confident angler is then free to concentrate on the important elements of fishing the right water in the correct manner.

So if you are new to steelhead angling, how do you choose your confidence flies? Pragmatic as it may sound, just ask around. Seek the advice of your friends who fish steelhead. If you take a guided trip, consult with your guide or with fly shop personnel. Or peruse my own list, included herein. No matter how you proceed in choosing the flies you will trust, keep the number of patterns to a minimum, at least for a while. Concentrate more on perfecting your angling skills.

Many experienced steelhead anglers eventually decide that fly choice should proceed under the auspices that the way in which we hook a steelhead counts for more than our final tally. My closest steelheading friends, for example, prefer to say, "I fished the pool well," rather than relate our body count. We all enjoy the thrill of the hookup, and we fish beautiful flies because doing so heightens our sense of what is right about our chosen sport. Our best efforts at the vise and on the river pay homage to a gamefish whose remarkable life story demands, in our opinion, a deep reverence and continual wonderment.

Indeed they are wondrous, wonderful fish, these steelhead and willing to humor us by chasing our bejeweled flies, all the while proving too mysterious in their behaviors for us to figure out entirely. Perhaps that's what endears them to us.

POPULAR FLIES

If we could characterize the classic steelhead fly it would assuredly be one of the traditional hairwing flies, once regularly called bucktails. Included are many of the patterns that have proven both their effectiveness and their popularity for many decades—flies such as the Skunk, Green-Butt Skunk, Purple Peril, Skykomish Sunrise, and Golden Demon. The list of these traditional flies includes many dozens of patterns, many of which have faded into obscurity.

Then come the later arrivals, such as the so-called "Spey flies," which are defined by their long-fibered hackles wound through the body. The original Spey flies date to the nineteenth century on the River Spey in northeast Scotland, but steelhead anglers have embraced, emulated, and modified the style since the 1950s, led by the creative and talented Syd Glasso, who hailed from Washington's Olympic Peninsula. Our list of steelhead flies would then expand to include dry flies, featherwing flies, and other flies defying easy classification.

Over time, many experienced steelhead anglers tend to narrow their selection of flies to the point that each angler relies overwhelmingly on just a few patterns. The flies listed below enjoy proven track records and serve faithfully as the "confidence flies" for many anglers. You can't go wrong in choosing them; nor can you hinder your fortunes astream by devising your own list of go-to patterns that includes none of those I have selected.

I rely primarily on several classic flies, on patterns of my own design, and on flies devised by my longtime fishing partner, Forrest Maxwell. My favorites include the Spawning Purple, Maxwell's Purple Matuka, Black Max, Brad's Brat, Cummings Special, and Orange Heron. Like most fly tiers I subject all of these dressings to endless variations.

Significantly, any steelhead fly must be properly dressed so as to fish in the correct manner. Wet flies should sink below the surface and remain there even under tension from a floating line. Dry flies designed to skate on the surface must be extremely buoyant but also reasonably easy to cast.

Wet Flies

Skunk
Black Max
Brad's Brat
Maxwell's Purple Matuka
Skykomish Sunrise

Green-Butt Skunk
Cummings Special
Purple Peril
Spawning Purple
Orange Heron

Spawning Purple

Skunk

Skykomish Sunrise

Cummings Special

Maxwell's Purple Matuka

Black Max

Purple Peril

Polar Shrimp

Brad's Brat

Spey-Style Steelhead Flies

Weighted Flies

Boss (top) and Orange Comet

Dry Flies

Grease-Liner
Steelhead Muddler

Bomber

Bomber

Keep the hook sharp.

4

THE WET FLY SWING

"The main idea is to let the fly race across current, across that particular slick or riffle where after a long, long while you somehow know Old Dynamite is waiting."

—Syl MacDowell, 1948

The wet fly swing, the basic steelheading technique, derives from a centuries-old method of fly angling for Atlantic salmon. The basic idea is to cast downstream and across, mend upstream to straighten the line and leader (not always necessary), and then allow the fly—under tension from the current—to swing back to your side of the flow.

In short, you make the fly drag. We spend most of our trout fishing days learning to eliminate that evil thing called drag. No wonder steelheading is so easy: We *want* the fly to drag. Throw the fly down and across, mend once, and allow the fly to drag back to your side of the river. Take two steps downstream and repeat. Pretty simple.

It's a matter of covering as much water as possible during the course of a day, hence the cast-swing-step approach that gives every available fish at least one chance to see the fly. Most of the time, if a steelhead wants to chase it, she'll do so at the first opportunity.

Wet Fly Swing

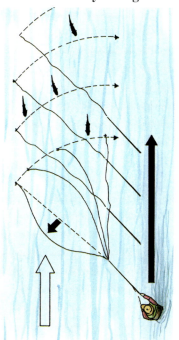

LEFT: Move downstream one or two steps between casts.
RIGHT: Begin the wet fly swing by casting at approximately a 45-degree angle across the current (far left). An immediate upstream mend (second from left) allows the fly to sink and dead-drift for a few feet before the line comes taut. As the current tightens the line and sweeps it down and across, the fly follows, swinging across the stream (third from left). You may need to make additional mends to control the speed and depth of the fly. At the end of the swing, the line hangs downstream (far right). Take one or two steps downstream, make another cast, and repeat the process.

That's why—unless perhaps you are covering visible fish—you want to keep moving.

The learned British author John Ashley-Cooper, in his book *The Salmon Rivers of Scotland,* could as easily have been discussing western steelheading when he wrote:

"In big pools, and in these rivers the majority of them are big, you should normally fish quickly, especially when fish are scarce. On no account pause to do two or three casts in the same place (this is almost an endemic fault in nervous waders). This leads to a deplorable waste of time. Keep moving on steadily at a rate of two or three yards between each cast and so get the water covered. Only if you locate a spot where likely takers

The wet fly swing: The angler casts down and across stream (above) and allows the fly to swing back to his side of the river (page 67).

FLY FISHING FOR STEELHEAD

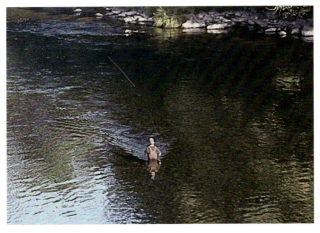

The fly is now directly downstream of the angler.

are lying, or if you rise fish that do not take hold, should you slow up. It is much better to fish a big pool twice, fairly fast, in a given period of time than once, slowly."

Specific current structures dictate the angle of the downstream cast, but generally speaking, the steeper the angle, the easier it becomes to control the fly's speed as it swings across the flow.

In fact, the speed of the fly and its depth in the water column comprise the two critical elements in steelhead presentation. When fishing floating lines and wet flies during the summer, fly depth more or less takes care of itself, especially when you control the more important element of fly speed. Steep angles of presentation and some timely mending control the speed of the fly. In short, a slow, controlled swing accounts for more

Using a steep angle of presentation, this angler swings the fly through the seam between the bank and the rapids.

hookups than a fly zipping rapidly back across the river.

Controlling depth and speed becomes a more critical issue with winter steelhead, which won't chase down a fly as aggressively as will summer-run fish. Thus, you must present the fly closer to the steelhead's level. You needn't dredge the bottom, but you must swing the fly deeper in the water column, often just a foot or two above the streambed.

A couple tricks help with fly control during winter: First, you can hold a large loop of line in your hand during the swing and steadily release this slack line to slow the fly's speed and thus increase its depth. Second, try stepping downstream after the cast rather than before. In summer, the typical pattern is to fish out one swing, take a step or two downstream, and then cast again. During the winter, however, try fishing out one swing and then making the next cast from the same position. After making the cast, take those two steps downstream, allowing the line a few more feet of drag-free drift to gain depth.

Another trick is to cast down and across, but at the end of the cast leave the rod tip elevated in preparation for a quick stack mend. In other words, as soon as the fly touches down, make a quick roll cast, shooting a loop of line that rolls the floating portion of the fly line partway out. This stack mend gives you a few feet of slack line—and thus dead drift—that helps the sinking portion of the line gain depth before the fly begins to swing.

Your choice of casting stations often dictates the methods used to control fly speed and the degree to which these methods prove effective. An often over-looked pool on one of our local rivers exemplifies the importance of the angler's position: Located at the lip current, deep in the tail-out of a much larger pool, a narrow pocket in the bedrock allows migrating steel-head a respite after negotiating the falls immediately below.

We can fish this slot from either side of the river, but only if we position ourselves above and within a rod's length laterally of the pool. In other words, we stand almost directly upstream from the holding area. Try to fish the slot from a steeper angle, and the fly and line either latch onto ledge rock or dash across the pocket so quickly as to render the presentation ineffective.

I could cite countless similar examples. In short, the steeper your angle of presentation, the easier it becomes to control the speed of the fly without mending. The importance of fishing at steep angles may be the best justification for casting a long line on large western rivers. Basically, it's a matter of geometry. When thrown at identical down-and-across angles from the same position, the longer cast covers a wider swath of water *at the appropriate speed* than does a shorter cast.

Initial positioning in the pool allows you to fish the best possible angle of presentation, but rod position and rod movement also play critical roles in fly control. You can either follow the fly or lead the fly with the rod, depending again on particular current structures in relation to the path of the line and fly. Following the fly means that once the line straightens, you keep the rod tip pointed out over the river. Doing so allows you direct contact throughout the presentation and gives you the opportunity to hang the fly in particular places, at least toward the end of the crosscurrent swing.

One of my favorite local pools perfectly illustrates the principle of following the fly. The pool features a major current seam well out in the flow, formed by a huge submerged slab of rock. Steelhead often hold on the far side of the seam in the slower water thirty feet below the rock. To present the fly effectively to these fish, you must cast well across the flow and then make a big upstream mend. Then you must hold the rod tip as far out toward the middle of the river as possible so the fly can come around and begin its swing in or near the seam. If you fail to do this, the fly darts through the seam as the current pulls it quickly to your side of the river. (See diagrams.)

Leading the fly, meanwhile, is a technique that can help slow the fly in swift currents or help speed it through slow currents. A slow-moving fly is good; an *un*moving fly is not so desirable. So in some cases you may need to lead the fly with rod tip—in effect using the rod and line in conjunction with the currents to pull the fly through slow water. Or in some cases you might lead the fly to slow its speed by allowing the rod tip to drift downstream slightly faster than the fly. Doing so causes the fly to swing across stream in a more angled arc—a valuable ploy when you can't get a steep enough angle on a narrow slot well out in the flow. (See diagrams.)

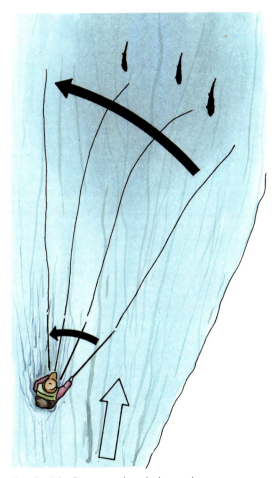

"Leading" the fly across a broad, slow pool.

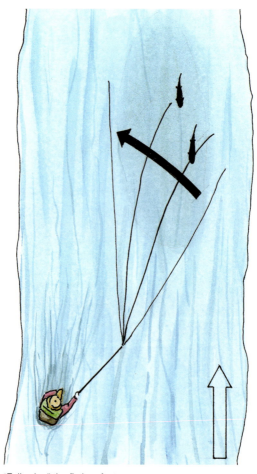

"Following" the fly in a fast, narrow run.

FLY FISHING FOR STEELHEAD

Regardless of the particulars of your presentation, success ultimately hinges on your ability to fish the fly in the proper place. In other words, reading a river and identifying the likely holding water rank as the most significant factors in determining your ability to hook fish consistently. In some rivers, the good pools are so well known that you need only watch for other anglers. Still, learning such pools yourself allows you to find the sweet spots in any given stretch of water.

Meanwhile, each day spent fishing adds to your arsenal of skills. As I have said, the basic technique for steelhead fly angling is decidedly easy to learn and execute. Yet there remains ample room for skill to prevail over a common flogging of the water, and fly control lies in that realm of skills in which we should tirelessly aim to improve.

EXECUTING THE SWING

Begin fishing at the upstream extent of the pool or run (this is called the head of the pool), where the riffle or rapids above feeds into slower, softer, deeper currents. Strip from the reel a few yards of line and begin with a short cast aimed down and across stream. Allow the current to pull the line taut, swinging the fly back to your side of the river until it hangs in the current directly downstream. Now strip two more yards of line from the reel and repeat the same cast. We call this "fishing out the short casts." These first few casts cover the water closest to you and cannot be neglected.

The author swings a fly through a typical steelhead run.

Lengthen the line by about two yards on each successive cast until you have arrived at the maximum amount of line you need or want to cover the water. Then, instead of lengthening the line, take two steps between casts, fishing out each cast and stepping downstream before making the next presentation. Continue in this manner until you have fished down through the length of the pool or run.

On some rivers—Oregon's North Umpqua offers the perfect example—many pools must be fished from a single casting station or from a few such stations. (This is called "station-to-station" fishing.) Some pools are essentially impossible to wade from top to bottom, the water typically being too deep or otherwise inaccessible. So anglers choose a particular rock,

Casting down and across to present the fly on the swing.

During the swing, the rod usually points downstream.

ledge, gravel bar, or position on shore from which to cover as much of the pool as possible.

In these cases, you simply lengthen the line by two yards or so with each successive cast until you have either covered all the water, or covered all you can reach. In the station-to-station pools, start at the uppermost casting station, cover all the water you can reach, then reel in, move downstream to the next station, and begin the process anew.

Whether you're wading through the pool or casting from stations, learn to minimize false casts. The fewer false casts, the more quickly you deliver each successive presentation, thereby covering the pool as efficiently as possible. Each false cast you eliminate adds one more fishing cast that day, and the more casts you make the more chances you have of presenting the fly to a biter.

Properly executed, the swing technique develops a beautiful, efficient rhythm: You cast, fish out the swing, strip in a little line, pick up the line, turn the cast back out over the river with the first false cast, and deliver the next fishing cast immediately. Practiced steelheaders make the wet fly swing seem like a well-ordered dance routine.

THE IMPORTANCE OF LINE CONTROL

When you chase steelhead—especially summer-run fish—on the big western rivers, you need to cover water and cover it effectively. Reading and covering water are the two most important aspects of fly angling for these wonderful gamefish. Much of the available literature talks about different kinds of casts and mends, often ascribing them fancy names like "stack mend." Yet even myriad, carefully categorized casting and mending techniques cannot begin to address the immense variety of real-life, on-the-river fishing situations. After all, every steelhead pool offers its unique nature, its particular structure and flow. Such characteristics affect the location and behavior of steelhead in that pool and thereby determine our tactical approach.

Because of the unique characteristics of each steelhead run or pool, I find it rather limiting to teach particular line-control skills in context with specific water types. Instead, I like to teach instinctive steelheading: Learn to cast, mend, and control line; learn to read a steelhead river. Then use whatever combination of learned and off-the-cuff skills you need to swing or swim your fly as slowly as possible across the pool. Most anglers, once they understand the virtue of controlling fly speed, easily learn to instinctively manipulate the line and the presentation.

Occasionally we find pools called "self-menders." Such pools require nothing in terms of line control beyond the cast itself. Self-menders are arranged so perfectly that they do everything for you: They straighten the line and they swim the fly at the perfect speed. Mending the line is wasted effort and might even cost a hookup.

At the other extreme are the complex pools where the initial cast must be delivered specifically to set up a subsequent series of mends. One of my favorite pools, in fact, offers a productive slot that requires an across-stream cast delivered with an upstream reach so that the fly lands slightly downstream of the line. At the same time, I must complete the cast with a high stop so the rod and line are positioned for an immediate, underpowered roll cast that positions a loop of slack line upstream from the fly. All this is done just to set up the fly for a nice, controlled swing through the bottom of the slot.

A few years ago I had the chance to introduce some Midwesterners to a big western steelhead river replete with complex pools. Standing on a rock beside one such pool, I pointed out the sweet spot where the fish was likely to take if indeed a steelhead occupied the run. One of the fellows, Dave, accepted the challenge. The cast alone covered eighty feet, but Dave was equal to the task. He wasn't mending the line quite right, however, so the fly, even when it landed in the right place, darted away too quickly. I yelled instructions from atop my perch: "Put it in the same place again, Dave . . . Perfect, okay, now mend upstream, quick, and hold your rod tip out toward the slot."

Soon the light went on. Dave saw how an incorrect presentation caused the fly to dart out of the soft water that offered the only haven for a steelhead. No steelhead would chase a fly into the rushing white water immediately adjacent to the little slot, so the angler had to hang the fly in the slow water long enough to draw a reaction. Quite suddenly my friend, who had honed his skills on streams of a different nature, un-

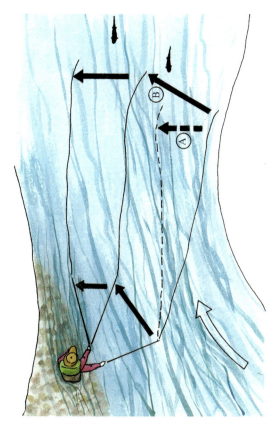

Here the angler leads the fly to slow its progress through the flow. In this fast, narrow seam, the angler cannot gain a steep enough angle of presentation to "follow" the fly, so the second-best option is to allow the rod tip to swing downstream slightly faster than the drift of the fly. This causes the fly to swing in a wide downstream arc (B) rather than a narrow arc straight across the flow (A).

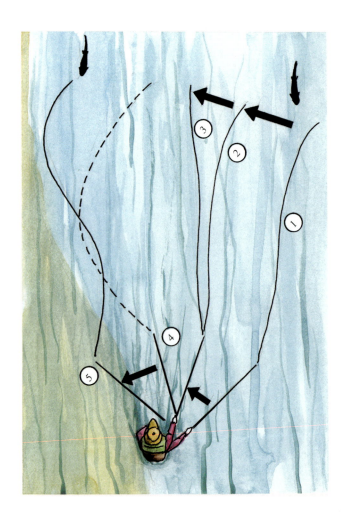

derstood why I had admonished him all day to swing the fly slowly through the pools.

Dave finally got one just right: perfect cast, perfect mend, and perfect rod position. Just as the fly straightened into the slot, I yelled, "Now that cast deserves a fish."

Wham! Fish on. Dave landed a beautiful native buck, and of course I was worshiped as some kind of divining fish god. My partners failed to realize, of course, that I mutter that same phrase, at least to myself, every time I make a decent cast. Save some knowledge of the pool on my part, it was Dave's ability to depart from his normal thought processes and make the perfect cast and presentation that earned him that fish.

"Backmending" is another method of mending line to the downstream (or inside) side of the fly, but in this case the mend is used to extend the swing into good holding water located between the angler and the near bank. (Normally the angler would wade inside of all the good water, but in this example the angler wades aggressively to cover the good water, knowing that at the lower end of the pool the current pushes toward the left-hand bank and the water deepens on that side.) The angler casts down and across (1) and allows the rod and fly to swing down and across (2). Soon the fly hangs directly below the angler (3) and stops swinging. To fish the potentially productive water to the inside, the angler can either flip a mend to the inside (4) or switch hands with the rod and point the tip down toward the near bank (5), causing the fly to swing in that direction.

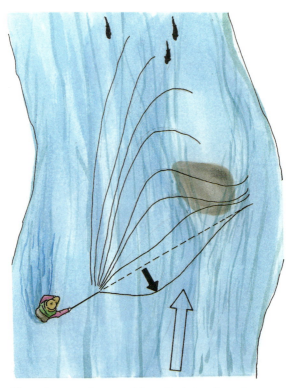

These diagrams show one of the author's favorite pools, where the angler must hold the rod out over the river throughout most of the presentation to get the proper swing. LEFT DRAWING—CORRECT: If the angler reaches the rod across stream and holds it there, the fly comes around and begins to swing effectively while still within the current seam created by the submerged boulder.

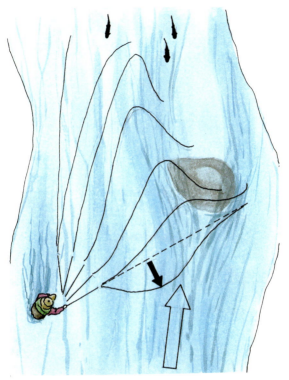

RIGHT DRAWING—INCORRECT: If the angler allows the rod to drift downstream, the fly gets held up in the slow water while the line bellies badly in the fast water. Consequently the fly darts straight downstream, pulled along by the fly line, and doesn't begin a controlled swing until it drifts beyond the current seam at midriver.

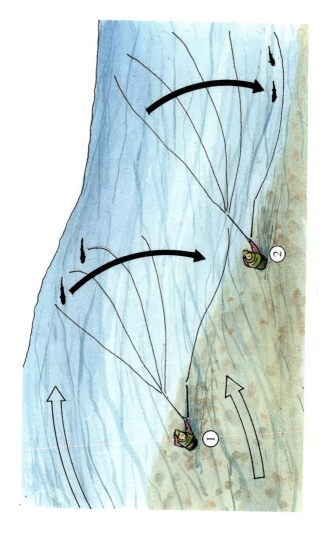

FLY FISHING FOR STEELHEAD

Later, as we ate dinner, Dave and I talked about the nature of that presentation. The configuration of the river dictated his choice in line control: A fast current ran a path straight through the middle of the river, which here was bounded on both sides by ledge rock. The far bank offered a narrow slot, where a seam in the current offered ideal holding water against a rock ledge. This slot—just a bathtub-sized, miniature pool—was unfishable unless an angler stood on a narrow gravel berm way up at the head of the fast water.

The long cast dropped the fly atop the slot. An upstream flip and loft positioned all of the fly line above the fly and well to the left of the current. The angler's position left him at the steepest possible angle to the pool, and he held his rod out to the left and kept it there as the line came taut. Combined with his initial positioning, Dave's cast, mend, and rod position allowed him to dance the fly slowly through the narrow slot. No written labels describe the presentation that earned Dave his fish—it was an instinctive reaction to the structure of the pool. Once Dave understood why the fly had to swing slowly through the little pool, he simply

This diagram shows one of the author's favorite pools that requires the angler to first "follow" the fly (1) and then "lead" the fly (2) with the rod tip on each presentation. A cobblestone bar extends to midriver and then drops off, creating ideal steelhead water. But owing to the curvature of the current structure, the angler must swing the rod to the downstream side at the end of each presentation to make the fly swing in toward the drop-off, where fish often hold.

flew by the seat of his pants and did what needed doing. I was yelling instructions, sure, but Dave's fishing instincts translated my simple instructions ("Okay, now mend!") into the perfect presentation.

CONFIDENCE COUNTS

Steelhead fly anglers constitute a decidedly twisted lot. We have little choice in the matter because our chosen pastime assures that we spend far more time fishing than actually catching. We operate on faith, on the assumption that if we just keep fishing we will, sooner or later, hook a steelhead.

Here in the Northwest, most of us fish big water—the Deschutes, Skykomish, Thompson, North Umpqua, Clearwater, Skagit, and many more. For some of these rivers you can watch the fish counts at the dams and garner at least some rough guess as to how many steelhead have migrated up to your favorite reaches. Even so, you simply assume that each pool holds fish, because only rarely on these rivers can one actually spot fish in the water.

Your faith must never falter. You must always believe that fish are in the river, in your favorite pools, and in a mood to chase your flies. In fact, confidence may well constitute the single most important attribute of the successful steelhead angler.

Confidence transcends technique and strategy. More than that, confidence elevates your angling skills because it instills in you a belief that there exists no doubt about the fact that you will hook a steelhead.

Not burdened by doubt, you come to decide that casting, wading, and reading water are skills at which you will tirelessly try to better yourself.

Any doubts about hooking steelhead are pushed far out of your mind. As you deliver a cast, there exists not a shred of doubt that a steelhead will grab the fly on that presentation. When this fails to happen, you are at the very least mildly surprised. Your confidence doubles on the ensuing cast—after all, if the last cast failed to tempt a fish, there is simply no question that the next one is sure to score. When this next presentation goes fishless, you find yourself quite flabbergasted, and when you fish out the pool without touching a fish you are entirely astounded.

Your astonishment only redoubles your confidence. No question about it: You will certainly hook a fish in the next pool. Should the day pass without a hookup, you find yourself brimming with confidence about your chances the following day. Should a week pass without a hookup, your confidence has reached epic proportions: It builds in direct proportion with your astonishment over not catching fish.

Never does your confidence wane; rather it follows this inverse relationship, mounting appreciably with the passage of fishless casts, pools, and days. Your reasoning is simple, fundamental. How can there exist any doubt that the next cast will hook a steelhead, since the last five hundred have failed to do so?

Indeed, doubt never enters the confident steelheader's mind. In this way you become a better angler, concentrating fully on your efforts. When your fly hangs in the current directly downstream at the end of the swing, you stand there entirely befuddled that a steelhead did not give chase. Then you can't wait to deliver the next presentation, because you are more certain than ever that the forthcoming cast will hook a fish.

The confident steelheader, unencumbered by doubt, appreciates that reading water and effectively covering water rank as the two most significant factors in hooking fish. The confident angler never worries over pat-

A beautiful wild summer steelhead caught with the wet fly swing.

tern choice. He chooses a favorite, ties it on, and forgets about the fly. The confident angler believes in every pool and fishes each one from top to bottom, knowing full well that giving up even one cast short of the lip current might spell the difference between success and failure.

Unburdened by worries, the steelhead angler now begins to appreciate the fact that few angling pursuits place him in more intimate quarters with a favorite river. As the seasons mount and the wading and casting miles add up; as those cherished hookups become many; as lifelong angling friendships are forged; as new rivers become old stomping grounds, the steelhead angler learns that he persists in this game simply because he loves to fish and because these noble gamefish and the rivers in which they live deserve a special reverence.

5

FISHING THE SUMMER RUNS

"The summer steelhead is a sport fish of superlatives—the only comparable freshwater rival being the Atlantic salmon."

—Bill McMillan, 1979

TIMING THE RUNS

Summer-run steelhead ascend rivers in the Northwest between late spring and late autumn, the precise timing of the runs varying from place to place. One river's run might peak during July, while the runs in another river don't reach a peak until October. Much depends on the location of the river in question, with those closest to the ocean nearly always peaking earlier than those far inland, but each river's steelhead populations have evolved differently.

Oregon's Rogue River, for example, enjoys its largest runs of summer steelhead in mid-autumn, yet the Rogue feeds directly into the Pacific. These are primarily steelhead of half-pounder life history, like those on California's Klamath. They smolt during late spring, spend a few months in salt water, and return to the river as immature fish that very autumn. Most half-pounders depart the river yet again and return a second time as small adults. Regardless of their specific life histories, these small steelhead truly comprise an autumn run of summer fish.

A bright summer steelhead.

Conversely, the rivers on Washington's Olympic Peninsula peak during June and July, as the fish enter these waters much earlier in the year. Distance has a lot to do with it on many rivers: Summer steelhead bound for eastern Washington and western Idaho arrive there during late summer and autumn—their journey up the Columbia and Snake rivers takes weeks or even months.

Idaho anglers, fishing the Clearwater and Salmon rivers between December and March, sometimes refer to "winter steelheading." In this case, the term defines a time of year and not a race of fish, for all the steelhead in the upper Columbia and Snake River drainages are by definition summer-run steelhead. They arrive in their home rivers in the fall and then winter over,

Jennifer Byers with a fine summer steelhead.

continuing their migration to the spawning grounds (if they are natives) during early spring.

But throughout the coastal belt of California, Oregon, Washington, and British Columbia, "winter steelheading" is generally understood to denote fishing for the winter-run race of fish.

Water conditions might also dictate the timing of certain steelhead runs. In northern California, for example, most adult summer steelhead depart salt water between late April and June. If these fish wait any longer, they risk encountering stream flows already too low and warm for safe passage to the upper tributaries where they wait out the heat of summer before continuing on to the spawning streams. Similarly, the inland steelhead bound for the Snake River tributaries often find unfavorably warm water when they arrive during August and September and are thereby compelled to seek deep, cool pools on the Snake until autumn brings cooler flows to their natal rivers.

In any event, with steelhead timing is everything. You must fish when the fish are in the river and while they are in prime condition. You might find a few fish in Oregon's Deschutes River during June and early July, but the run peaks between August and October, so most steelheaders fish the river during those months. Those same fish still inhabit the river in January and February, but their presence there in late winter does not necessarily mean that they represent a legitimate pursuit for fly anglers. The wild fish among them will be near spawning, and the rules of fair chase dictate that we leave them be at that time of year.

FISHING THE SUMMER RUNS

So steelhead anglers must determine the window of opportunity for any given river. On most summer-run waters, the season lasts for several months, allowing ample opportunity for fly anglers to ply their craft. Dedicated anglers learn to anticipate the seasonal patterns on their favorite rivers. For example, my local river fishes well between mid-June and mid-September, so for three months I needn't go elsewhere. When the action slows in mid-September, I venture to the Deschutes and North Umpqua rivers, both of which fish well through the month of October. Anywhere in the Pacific Northwest, steelhead addicts pursue similar schedules that allow them to learn the intricacies of their favorite waters.

EARLY AND LATE

Certainly the early morning and the magical evening hours rank as the best times to be on the water during your pursuit of summer steelhead. First thing in the morning I like to fish shallow tail-outs, especially on my home river. Migrating fish often travel upriver at low light and then settle into a flat, shallow tail-out where they remain until the first boat or first wading angler spooks them into better cover.

Even though I love early morning and evening fishing, I don't mind the midday hours, and on my local river there flows an elegant, broad, elbow-bend pool whose productive waters exemplify the game of midday summer steelheading. By late August, with the water at its lowest point of the year, the gear anglers and most of the fly anglers abandon this pool. They assume the water is too low for the fish to hold there.

That's when I like this pool the best. The low water allows me to wade the river and fish the pool from the far bank. Several depressions on that side offer refuge for the fish, and they hold in those places all summer. At the tail-out is a tiny lip-current pool, no larger than a bathtub. But I don't bother getting here at first light. Here's where local knowledge helps. No boats will float over this spot until at least midday, because the nearest launch is several miles upriver. Meanwhile, tall alder trees cast long shadows over the tail-out until about 10 AM.

Given the circumstances, I don't bother with this pool until midmorning. My time is better spent fishing other water, and nothing is as rewarding as tempting a banker's-hours thirty-incher from the glassy shallows of this run during late August. So don't give up on the high-sun hours. If more anglers fished at midday, more steelhead would be taken at midday. It's that simple.

VARY YOUR APPROACH

Low, clear water dictates a quiet, careful approach, right? Well, maybe. Certainly trout anglers must approach with care under such conditions—but steelhead don't necessarily behave like trout. Sometimes you have to wake them up. During the summer, I often make two passes through a pool. On the first pass, I assume a conservative strategy of wading shallow and

The author battles a fresh-run fish in June.

casting delicately. On the second pass, though, I abandon such concerns. Steelhead often seem to wake up
after an angler wades and fishes through a pool.
Hence, the second angler through gets the hookup.

Jim Teeny once talked of throwing rocks in the river
to awaken dour fish. I'll readily admit to having tried
that approach. Mostly, though, I simply count on my
wading and casting to do the job. Better yet, I'll let
somebody else do the job for me. Give me one pass
through an undisturbed run and that's all I want of vir-
gin water. After that first pass, I'll just about beg a boat
to float through or another angler to fish through. In
either event, I'm hitching up the waders, heading for
deep water, and fishing through aggressively.

I can't even count the number of times unproductive water turned suddenly bountiful after something disturbed the pool. Some years ago I was fishing Washington's diminutive Kalama River under a brutal August sun. All day I'd done little more than practice my casting. About three in the afternoon I stood above a glassy pool, watching three dour steelhead gently fanning their broad tails to maintain position deep in a tail-out. I'd fished this water earlier with no results.

As I watched from the guardrail above, a lone drift boat tried desperately to negotiate the narrow channel with its myriad rocks exposed by the low water. The boat drifted right over the fish, and still they held their position. Immediately thereafter came a nasty, metallic, fingernails-on-chalkboard grinding noise as the boat skidded off a boulder. Immediately all three steelhead dashed upstream into the choppy water at the head of the pool, where they disappeared from sight. I hustled up to the top of the pool and within minutes was fast to an eight-pounder.

THE EARLY SUMMER

The first summer-run steelhead arrive in coastal rivers during May and June. They tend to be speed demons, using the high flows to head deep into the river systems where they will remain for many months before winter rains provide access to spawning tributaries. So long as the flows remain at early summer levels, fly anglers might need to persist in using winter-type tactics to enjoy much hope of success.

Generally this means sink-tip lines and slow, controlled swings that fish the fly deeper in the flow than is required for steelhead under better conditions. For the particulars, study Chapter 6.

THE DOG DAYS

Many dedicated steelhead enthusiasts, myself included, embrace the dog days of late summer. We relish those hot August days when reports of dour fish keep most anglers home mowing the lawn. But we also make the necessary adjustments by fishing different kinds of water, fishing different strategic patterns, and making a few tactical adjustments in our presentations.

During periods of low, clear, warm water, some steelhead invariably take refuge in shallow, choppy

The author with a trophy-class Oregon summer steelhead.

water—places you can ignore earlier in the summer. But shallow riffles at the top ends of pools and runs rank as prime spots to fish for steelhead in late summer. In such places the fish find oxygenated cool water. More important, perhaps, they find cover. The choppy, broken surface offers the ultimate form of camouflage when the glassy pools below become so skinny that you can count every fish.

The typical steelhead run features good holding water at the head, or upstream extent of the pool, where the current first begins to slacken and where the river gains depth. Normally you start at the head, fishing through water about hip deep or deeper. In late summer, however, start even higher. Fish the choppy, one- to two-foot-deep riffle water at the uppermost end of

Casting over gin-clear water in midsummer.

the run. Amid the chop, look for current seams trailing down behind rocks and gravel bars. Hang a fly in these places even if most of the water seems to flow faster than the water you're accustomed to fishing. I'm never surprised anymore to find late-summer steelhead holding in these shallow, choppy glides, yet most steelhead anglers pass over such unlikely looking places.

Far more obvious are the effects of shade. Late-summer steelheaders actively look for shaded water during the middle of the day. Shaded water allows for slightly cooler water temperatures than are found in the exposed, sun-baked pools. More significant, perhaps, shade allows steelhead to see your fly during those midday periods of blinding sunlight.

Jennifer Byers fishes the evening light.

FLY FISHING FOR STEELHEAD

On some rivers, steelhead become horribly difficult to rise at midday. Oregon's Deschutes River is the perfect example. The Deschutes runs south to north, so the fish spend most of their time looking directly into the sun. In the morning and evening, Deschutes steelhead enjoy ample shade from the river's steep canyon walls. But when the sun hits the water, the fish are effectively blinded. At the same time, they feel exposed and vulnerable, so many of these fish abandon shallow lies and seek deeper or sheltered water.

Steelhead in other rivers rise often in bright sun, so long as the angler exercises some foresight in choosing his or her tactics. My local river is a good midday river. Certainly morning and evening account for most of the dry-line hookups, but those who persist during midday catch plenty of steelhead in bright sunlight. When the sun is high in the sky, fish from the south bank when possible. This allows the fly to swing in from the north, where it is more visible than if swinging in with the sun from the south.

As afternoon progresses, seek pools that flow somewhat east to west or north to south, so the sun is behind the fish. Think about it this way: If the sun is in your face as you fish down through a pool, then the sun is behind the fish. Just like us, steelhead see a lot better without a bright sun angled directly into their faces. Also, fish the choppy runs. The broken surface helps deflect the sun's direct glare, allowing the fish a better view of your incoming fly.

Sink-tip lines also help combat the glare of midday sun. As the sun climbs high into the sky, switch to the high-density sink-tip and shorten the leader to just four to six feet. The fly fishes a little deeper in the flow, below the worst of the glare, thereby giving the fish a better chance to track your offering.

In direct contrast to the traditional advice suggesting small flies for low water, I actually fish my usual array of large flies during the bright sun of midday. My reasoning is simple—if a blinding sun limits the fish's visibility, then certainly a big fly is easier to see than a small fly. Besides, larger flies tied on heavy-wire hooks fish slightly deeper on the swing, allowing them to penetrate the glare layer—those first few inches of water where the glare is at its worst.

The only time I switch to small flies is when I fish glass-smooth water where fly splash, or even line splash, might spook skittish steelhead. Under those conditions, especially at midday, I fish No. 6 and 8 patterns on ten- to twelve-foot leaders.

The bright sun of midday offers one last enticing advantage in the form of reduced fishing pressure. During late summer, everybody fights for the best water at dusk and dawn. But you won't have much competition on the water from noon to 4 PM on a 95-degree day. At times it seems the fish appreciate the break from the pressure as much as you might. I once spent an entire August morning shooting photographs on the North Umpqua's revered Camp Water. A constant parade of anglers fished through these storied pools and rose not a single fish all morning. By noon, the water lay completely abandoned. I retreated to the truck and exchanged camera for fly rod. An hour later I admired an awesome thirty-eight-inch buck that boiled for a Spawning Purple.

AUTUMN MAGIC

Autumn brings a new awakening to steelhead rivers. The breeze carries a subtle chill, and the season paints a wash of regal color over the streamside leaves. Water

Al Shewey fights a big summer-run fish in October.

temperatures drop a few degrees, and the steelhead stir and move and rediscover their early-season aggressiveness. On many waters, a smattering of fresh fish join those already in the river. This is the most magical time on most steelhead rivers, a time when the promise of low water and skated dry flies beckons the dedicated fly angler to abandon all other pursuits and head for favorite pools.

The autumn fishing continues through October and into November. By the first of December, earlier on some rivers and a little later on others, these summer-run fish have earned the right to be left unpursued. They will soon pool up in deep, slow water to wait out the remainder of the year until the winter rains spur them onward to the last stage of their migration into the spawning tributaries.

6

FISHING THE WINTER RUNS

"For winter steelhead . . . cover the water faithfully and well."

—Roderick Haig-Brown, 1947

They don't behave as endearingly as the summer fish that swim the rivers under perfect fly-rod conditions. Yet winter-run steelhead offer a charm all their own and an intrigue born of the rarity of each hookup. Certainly every dedicated fly angler can recount those days when hatchery-born winter steelhead pounced on

The author with a bright winter steelhead.

the fly all morning long. But even the hatchery fish are rarely so easily confronted as their summer brethren, and the big natives of late winter demand a dedication beyond that required to enjoy consistent success on summer steelhead.

Generally winter steelheading favors the gear angler, who can more easily combat high, cold water. Still, winter fish take flies readily if given the chance. Fly anglers must simply adjust their strategies and tactics to match the conditions. This means switching from floating lines to sinking lines, and sometimes weighted flies. Such tackle allows anglers to fish the fly deep enough in the flow to entice a winter steelhead to give chase. Then comes the important part:

A chrome-bright winter steelhead.

FLY FISHING FOR STEELHEAD

fishing the fly correctly in the right kind of water. Therein lies the inherent beauty of the classic wet fly swing, the same tactic employed to catch summer steelhead.

During winter, however, steelhead rarely move more than a few feet to attack a swinging fly. Anglers must swing the fly deeper and slower, and the angle of presentation is paramount in maintaining depth and controlling speed. In short, the steeper the angle of presentation, the more control you have over the fly.

On wide, cobblestone rivers where steelhead might hold anywhere from bank to bank, the best tactic is to cover as wide a swath of water as possible during each swing. So you follow the classic approach of quartering downstream and allowing the fly to swing all the way across the current. On more defined water, however, where you can expect the steelhead to hold in specific, narrow lies, you can make the cast more downstream than across and thus gain increased control over the speed and depth of the fly.

A couple of tricks help with fly control: First, you can hold a large loop of line in your hand during the swing and steadily release this slack line to slow the fly's speed and thus increase its depth. Second, try stepping downstream after the cast rather than before. During the summer, the typical pattern is to fish out one swing, take a step or two downstream, and then cast again. During the winter, however, try fishing out one swing and then making the next cast from the same position. After making the cast, take those two

Fishing a narrow run during good winter water conditions.

steps downstream, allowing the line a few more feet of drag-free drift to gain depth.

LINE SYSTEMS FOR WINTER STEELHEAD

The specific characteristics of the water dictate your choice in line systems. Fish a 400-grain shooting head on the North Umpqua's famous Boat Pool and you will likely lose a fly line to the submerged ledge rock. I've lost a few lines on the North Umpqua—enough to learn which pools fit my preferred style of fishing and which do not. On the other hand, my occasional March excursions to the Skykomish invariably lead me to a couple of favorite runs so devoid of obstructions that if the fly hangs up on small cobble at the end of the swing, a little slack line invariably frees the hook.

Steelhead anglers have benefited in recent years from the rapid growth in fly line technology. Each of the major line manufacturers now offers specialty lines designed for the conditions associated with winter steelhead angling. The most versatile of these are the multi-tip lines described in Chapter 2. With these lines, you can match the sinking tip to the water conditions, using the fastest-sinking, highest-density tips for deep and/or fast water, and the slower-sinking tips for shallow pools.

These multi-tip lines rely on small-diameter floating fly line, to which you attach the tip sections. They are similar in nature to shooting taper systems, except that the floating running line mends better than other varieties of running line. So in addition to matching the sinking capabilities of your line to the water's speed and depth, you should also decide whether the sink-tip line or the shooting taper systems better fit your water or your style of fishing.

Shooting tapers, or heads, require a slightly different approach. When backed up with monofilament or similar material as running line, high-density heads sink quickly: The running line offers minimal resistance at the surface when compared to the thin-diameter

The green-tinged water of winter.

floating fly line used on multi-tip lines. With the head system, you sacrifice the ability to mend line on the water, so you must execute the setup while the line is in the air.

Remember, the steeper the casting angle, the better you can control the fly. So lengthen out and cast long and steep on big water. As the head unfurls over the water, reach the rod upstream to allow for maximum dead-drift time. After the cast a hard, brief upstream pull on the rod aids in straightening the line and leader, giving you direct contact with the fly.

From time to time during the winter you may find opportunity to fish a floating line and a heavy fly across shallow tail-outs, even on big rivers. Many rivers will allow such tactics during the low-water periods of March or early April. The springtime sun warms the water slightly, making steelhead more aggressive. If warm, dry weather brings a drop in river levels, search out those shallow lips that hold winter steelhead in just two or three feet of water. Hooking winter steelhead on a floating line with a classic fly ranks among angling's most treasured rewards.

For such situations, you will want a reel loaded with a full-length floating fly line, giving you maximum ability to mend the line during the drift. By constantly tending to the line, you can slow the drift and swing enough that the fly maintains depth.

Fly Choices

The particular fly pattern matters little with regard to winter steelheading. The overriding concern, instead, is fly function. Above all you want the fly to sink easily. Heavily dressed patterns, overly adorned with fur and feather, tend to be slightly buoyant. They don't sink quickly. Conversely, sparsely dressed patterns offer less resistance, allowing the weight of the hook to carry the fly to depth. Some of the classic West Coast winter steelhead flies remain great choices for today's anglers. A study of Bill McMillan's Winter's Hope or Syd Glasso's Orange Heron reveals flies dressed with sparse application of materials on heavy-wire hooks.

A further option is to add weight to the fly. A plethora of "leech" flies adorn the fly bins at most shops, and most share the characteristic lead dumbbell eyes that quickly sink these patterns, especially when coupled with high-density fly lines. Older patterns, including the Comet flies, are equally effective and easier to cast than large, weighted, rabbit strip flies.

The type of water you fish often determines your choice in fly styles. For example, I like shallow, gliding runs and shallow, smooth tail-outs. In such places I can fish unweighted flies and easily fish deep enough to motivate a winter steelhead to give chase. I look for water to match my preferred style of fishing. The other

Fishing a classic run during winter.

FLY FISHING FOR STEELHEAD

option is to be versatile enough in your arsenal of tackle and flies to fish just about any kind of water you might encounter. That approach is equally acceptable and equally satisfying to those who make a specialty out of versatility.

TIMING IS EVERYTHING

Regardless of angling technique, your chances of hooking winter steelhead are directly proportional to the number of fish in the river and to the conditions you encounter when you get to the water. The general pattern in the Northwest is for the hatchery-produced one- and two-salt fish to arrive between December and February—depending on the specific river—and then for the big natives to arrive between February and mid-April. Many winter steelhead rivers offer both runs, while others host primarily one or the other. For example, Washington's spring catch-and-release season is aimed specifically at protecting the native steelhead, which arrive following the peak of the hatchery runs in rivers such as the Sauk, Skagit, and Skykomish. Oregon's North Umpqua, meanwhile, is a classic river for wild steelhead.

Timing the runs is one thing, and timing your trip to the river is another. Water conditions dictate your chances of success. Low flows afford the best opportunities for the fly angler, and while clear water is always nice, a slight tinge of green often signifies ideal conditions. The best water conditions tend to coincide with either cold, dry spells or extended warm, dry

Big, broad rivers, swollen with winter flows, can seem daunting.

spells. On many rivers, short bursts of warm weather often serve only to dirty the water with recent low-elevation snowmelt.

Anglers who wait around for perfect conditions can wait a long time. Every winter season is different on Northwest rivers. Some winters offer countless perfect days, while others afford but a precious few days when the water drops into shape. So fish when you can. Steelheading is a mathematical game: The more casts you make, the better your chances of finding a willing dance partner in the form of a chrome-bright winter steelhead.

7

SPECIALTY TACTICS

"Steelhead are rarely easy, and the angler who can adapt to varying conditions is going to be the most effective."

—Bill McMillan, 1979

SKATING DRY FLIES

Many steelhead anglers consider dry-fly fishing to represent the ultimate expression of their art, and indeed no other method can hope to match the heart-racing excitement of a huge fish boiling for a skated fly. Imagine a subtle evening breeze carrying hints of autumn chill and spiriting yellowing leaves from the riverside woods as you survey the promising folds of current curling through a quiet steelhead pool. Impenetrable to your searching eyes, the glassy surface glows green and gold, reflecting September's grasp on the river's forested canyon. The day's first few October caddis, an inch long and dressed for the season in a deep shade of orange, flutter about high over the river.

This is dry-fly time. You choose a pattern designed to roughly suggest the size and color of the giant caddisflies so familiar to the river and its inhabitants, though pattern rarely proves critical when a steelhead feels the need to smash a dry fly. Halfway through the run, a quartered-down cast draws tight and the fly plows a V-shaped wake while swinging across the even flows. You watch the fly intently as it traces a well-marked path across the pool.

With stunning, sudden ferocity a huge boil erupts behind the fly as a steelhead smashes the surface. He misses the fly, perhaps by design. The ripples begin to settle and suddenly the water wells up under the fly. The fish has chased again, but without breaking the surface. By now your hands are shaking visibly and you hardly dare breathe. The third rise is the telling strike, and the fish inhales the fly. Only your many years of swinging flies for steelhead provide you the discipline not to react, not to set the hook as you might with a rising trout. Instead you let the fish turn with the fly, and he is on.

Eventually you guide the beautiful fish to the protected shallows of a gravel bar and tail him in a foot of water, taking great care not to bring him too near shore, where he might bash himself against lethal rocks in his attempts to escape. The skater hangs limply from the corner of the steelhead's jaw—had the battle lasted much longer the hook would have pulled free. A narrow band of crimson marks the buck's flanks and gill plates, indicative of a fish regaining his troutlike colors during autumn.

The fish revives quickly and you usher him back to the cold, clean flows of his natal river. The experience will etch itself on your soul; you'll recount it many times among like-minded angling friends who nod in contemplative understanding. As Van Fleet wrote, this is what brings the steelhead addict back to the river year after year.

FLY FISHING FOR STEELHEAD

Angling with skated dry flies bears much in common with the usual wet fly/dry-line methods employed for summer-run fish. In both instances the down-and-across swing puts the fly in play, but with dry flies the entire experience is visible, so the only remaining concern is fly speed. As with wet flies, the general rule is to keep the fly working across the flow in a slow arc. Often, as in wet fly fishing, fly speed takes care of itself. At times, however, you must swing the rod toward the bank to lead the skated fly through dead spots in the current, or mend the line to gain better contact with the fly.

Jennifer Byers fishes pocket water for summer steelhead.

Surface flies go by several descriptive terms, including "waking fly," "skater," and "damp fly." In the verb form, you might be "skating," "waking," "riffling," or "skittering" your dry fly. These labels are essentially interchangeable, though the term "damp fly" is most often used to describe flies fished both on and immediately below, or "in" the surface. Damp flies (often Muddler patterns and derivations thereof) might fish dry on one cast and wet on the next, their depth entirely dependent on the conformation of the water's surface and the configurations of its current.

Damp flies and dry flies enjoy long-standing traditions, first in Atlantic salmon angling in Great Britain and much later in steelheading history. The great British Columbia–based angler Roderick Haig-Brown gave us the Steelhead Bee, and Walt Johnson enjoyed

Skating a dry fly on a smooth tail-out.

dry-fly success on Washington's North Fork Stillaguamish. But it was Harry Lemire, the legendary angler from Washington, who introduced many of us to the fine art of pursuing the sea-run rainbows with skaters. Lemire's Grease-Liner pattern was one of the first waking flies to earn widespread popularity, and it remains a staple to this day.

All waking flies, the Grease-Liner included, perform best when you fish them on flows ideally suited to dry-fly tactics. Such "skater water" combines a smooth surface with shallow water. These qualities abound on low-gradient steelhead rivers, but on steeper rivers you must seek the glassy tail-outs and smooth, gliding runs. Approach these pools cautiously, for shallow, clear, smooth water often holds skittish steelhead.

Ideal "skater water." Note the smooth surface and shallow flow.

A variety of skating flies.

GREASE-LINE TACTICS

The wet fly swing has its variations, including the so-called "grease-line" method, developed on Scotland's Aberdeenshire Dee early in the twentieth century. The essence of the grease-line technique is to present the fly broadside to the current. Proponents of the technique suggest that the fish, having benefited from a broadside view of the fly, will feel more inclined to strike than if the fly is presented in any other orientation.

I'm not convinced. After all, with its eyes situated on each side of the head like most fish, the steelhead enjoys exceptional vision of a wide arc on both sides. So if the fly arrives broadside from one side, its head pointed toward the bank (and the fish) the steelhead will first see it more or less head on. The swung fly, oriented more or less up- and downstream, probably gives as good or better a broadside profile as it swings in from the side.

In any event, the grease-line presentation begins with a cast made across or even slightly up and across. Then you make the initial mends to the upstream side to maintain the broadside dead drift. At some point you begin making mends to the downstream (shore-ward) side of the fly in an effort to extend the dead drift and to maintain the fly's broadside angle to the current. Finally you lead the fly across the flow in a gentle arc, continuing to mend downstream if needed to maintain the fly's orientation. No two pools fish exactly alike, so the number and types of mends you use varies frequently in response to the water you encounter. Ideally each mend or line movement repositions the line without disturbing the fly.

In highly practiced hands, the grease-line technique is a dance born of great skill in handling and manipulating both line and fly. The technique is best suited to calm waters on fairly small streams, or at least well-defined holding lies on big rivers.

I would contend that on large, complex rivers, any attempt to control the fly's actual orientation in the flow—whether the fly points upstream or across stream—is wasted energy. The fish seem unconcerned about such trivialities, and on long-line presentations, proponents of the "swimming" fly exert substantially less influence over the fly's attitude than they might believe.

SPECIALTY TACTICS

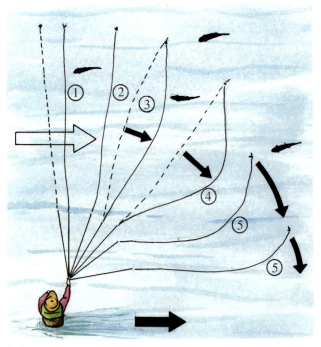

1. Cast and reach mend upstream.
2. Allow fly to dead-drift downriver.
3. Mend line to extend drift.
4. Continue mending to reposition the line downstream, so the fly remains broadside to the current.
5. Allow the fly to swing to a hanging-down position.

However, while I believe grease-line fishing to be no more or less effective than the classic swing, the technique is worth learning for several reasons. First, grease-lining mandates expertise in mending line and manipulating the drift without unnecessarily disturbing the fly. Such line control skills are valuable with all steelheading methods. Second, the across-stream cast often proves the best approach to skittish steelhead holding in shallow, clear water. When casting across stream rather than down, you ensure that line splash occurs well upstream from the fish. Finally, the grease-line approach often results in visible takes, and that fact along makes it worthwhile.

POCKET-WATER TACTICS

In many rivers steelhead, especially summer-run fish, often hold in pocket water characterized by myriad rocks and boulders forming numerous deep slots, seams, and miniature pools. The maze of conflicting currents and cascades often leaves ample room for the seagoing rainbows to find comfortable cover, and while this is hardly ideal fly water, the uppermost reaches of many rivers abound in such habitat and the fish utilize it readily.

Pocket water offers unique challenges, and successfully fishing such reaches demands skill in the always-important realms of line control and fly control. The classic dry-line swing, with a wet fly or skating dry fly, works quite nicely on the narrow runs and small pools found amid the boulders and white water of the typical pocket-water riffle or rapids. Fish a short line as often as possible so you can maintain control over the fly. A typical pocket-water cast might extend only fifteen to forty feet. Then think in terms of "mini-swings." Instead of swinging the fly all the way across a broad, classic pool, you will swing the fly across narrow holding areas, often just a few feet across.

A favorite reach of pocket water on my home river stretches for two hundred yards between a fine steelhead pool on the upstream end and a deep, slow salmon hole below. At low summer flows, I pick my way along the bank, dragging a wet fly through each of a dozen pockets that might hold steelhead. The largest of these requires but six or eight casts to cover it top to bottom, and several are one-cast slots where soft, deep seams border the main current.

Some of these pockets I fish from dry land, others from midstream after struggling through the jumble of boulders and tricky currents to gain an advantageous casting station. When I hook fish in this water I'm in for a wild ride. Rarely do they come to hand, for the swift water, littered with rocks of all sizes, gives the fish every advantage and most of them come unpinned in short order. But the excitement of each encounter encourages me to fish these pockets almost every time I visit that section of the river.

In addition to the typical pocket-water sections commonly found on the steep, upper reaches of summer-steelhead streams, many of our big, high-gradient rivers offer large rapids whose nearshore edges might offer ideal resting runs for migrating steelhead. Like many steelheaders, I always keep an eye peeled for such places as I walk the banks between the well-known runs and pools. A few casts here and there might just pay dividends. Still fresh in my memory is that September day years ago on the North Umpqua when I stopped to make a few exploratory casts in a pocket hidden amid modest rapids. I negotiated a deep channel to gain footing on a large slab of bedrock, delivered the first cast, and was caught flat-footed when a monstrous summer steelhead pounced on the fly and headed west like a runaway truck on a steep hill.

The author fishes an active retrieve to a steelhead he spotted in this small pool.

In a heartbeat he "went over" so to speak, departing the rapids and taking up stubborn refuge in the well-known pool impossibly far below. Miraculously my tackle held and the hook kept its grip while I forded the deep channel back to the bank, scurried

Small pools with even flows are ideal for grease-lining.

FLY FISHING FOR STEELHEAD

over rubble and brush for 150 yards, and finally caught up with the fish in quarters where we could properly do battle. Eventually I brought to hand a spectacular wild buck of thirty-six inches, the second-largest North Umpqua fish I've had the pleasure of releasing.

ACTIVE RETRIEVES

During the first half of the twentieth century, the Eel River and other northern California streams spawned their own unique regional method of steelhead fly angling. In order to effectively fish the slow-moving pools of the lower Eel, steelhead anglers there added an active retrieve to the usual wet fly swing. The water on the lower pools was so slow that the swinging fly hardly moved at all. So in order to entice often dour steelhead, the Eel River anglers stripped line during the swing. Still perhaps the best approach for fishing the meanders of the lower Eel, this technique soon spread to other rivers in California and southern Oregon.

The technique is easy to learn and simple to execute on the slow-moving pools where it works best. Make the initial cast across the flow and slightly downstream, and then mend to straighten the line and leader. Once the fly gains depth in the target area, begin stripping line with fairly slow, six- to eight-inch pulls. Continue doing so until the fly hangs directly below your position. Take a step or two downstream and repeat, and continue in this manner until you've covered all the good water.

Sometimes I employ the same technique in slow motion when fishing high-density sinking lines during winter. By slowly stripping line I am able to maintain direct contact with the fly. If I feel the fly begin dragging across a submerged rock or reef, I can prevent a snag by releasing a bit of line or in some cases making a quick pull on the line.

8

READING STEELHEAD WATER

"It is not obstinacy that draws anadromous fishes into difficult water. They cling to the main channel as a motorist follows highway pavement."
—Syl MacDowell, 1948

Steelhead occupy a wide variety of places in any given river. When asked precisely where to cast a fly, I answer as follows: "Look for water between the top of your knees and your eyebrows in depth, sometimes a little deeper, and which flows at about the pace you can walk."

A classic steelhead pool.

In other words, steelhead prefer water of moderate depth and moderate speed. Syl MacDowell, in *Western Trout*, summed up the matter eloquently when he defined steelhead water as "fast, shallow reaches where a moving fly is brought near enough this lord of the rainbows to overcome his indifference and to induce him to take it."

Both MacDowell's definition and my own seem simple enough but obviously they describe a vast amount of water on the average river. To narrow it down you must add a basic understanding of the nature of rivers and of how river characteristics influence the basic migratory habits of steelhead.

For starters, summer-run steelhead generally stick to the main current of the river. You won't find them in the frog water up near the banks. Also, the current structure and configuration of the river dictate where steelhead stop and where they don't. In short, they look for something comfortable. Forget about rapids. The water is too fast. Sometimes steelhead hold in pocket-water chutes and seams within a large rapids, but they are more prone to hold in the pools dividing the rapids, whether these pools take the form of broad, classic affairs or just narrow slots called "runs."

Any given pool can be divided into its parts: The head of the pool is that portion at the upstream end where the faster water above settles and slows. The body of the pool is the wide expanse at the middle, and the tail-out is the lower end, where the water often reaches its slowest speeds and shallowest depth, immediately above the next rapids or riffle.

Steelhead are also creatures of habit. Barring any major changes in the river's structure and flow, these fish utilize the same holding lies over and over, not only from day to day but from year to year. Therefore, steelhead anglers fish the same water religiously. If you hook a fish in a particular spot, remember that place—that exact place—and fish it in the future.

Not all holding lies are equal, or so it would seem. In any given run or pool, those places most preferred by the steelhead will hold a fish most often. Indeed, there exists an orderly ranking of sorts that occurs in many steelhead pools: If only one fish is present, that fish occupies the choice lie. If two fish are present, they occupy the two best lies. If three fish are present at a given time, they occupy those first two spots plus the third-best and so on.

Because our large western steelhead rivers rarely allow the angler to see his quarry, it makes strategic sense to fish each pool from top to bottom even if you know, for example, that the best holding lie—the place that most often produces a fish—awaits way down in the tail-out. If you don't know how many steelhead occupy the pool, always start at the top and fish over all the suspected or known lies. After all, the "garden spot" down in the tail-out isn't going anywhere, and you just might hook a fish from a place not typically as productive.

Armed with the knowledge that steelhead tend to follow the main current structure of the river and knowing they stop and hold, for varying time periods, in particular places, you must now begin to dissect the river. Steelhead orient to structure of various kinds,

Inside bends in the river create ideal holding water for steelhead.

ranging from single small rocks to ledges to gravel berms. If you can locate such structural elements within a pool or run, fish them carefully. On large rivers, you must learn to intimate the nature of the bottom by reading the water's surface. Large rocks leave telltale bulges and wakes; chutes leave slicks; ledges often create current seams, and so on.

Inside bends typically offer good steelhead water, but in this run the best water is found on the outside bend, owing to perfect current speed and ideal depths. Fish hold at the slot labeled (1), but further downstream on the bend the water is too shallow (2). The prime water in this run extends from the base of the rapids on the outside bend around the corner toward midstream (3 and 4). Area (5) is sufficiently deep, but too slow to hold fish. The final sure lie in this run is the tiny pocket (6) immediately above the small falls, where submerged ledge rock buffers the current, forming steelhead water of perfect speed and depth.

FLY FISHING FOR STEELHEAD

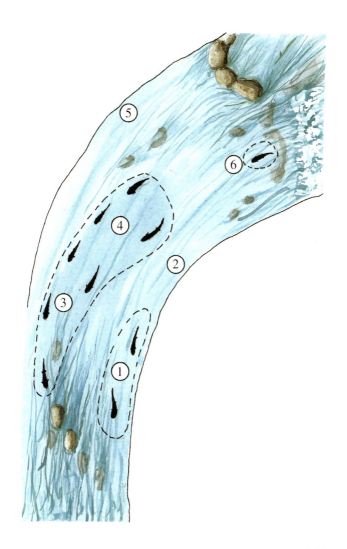

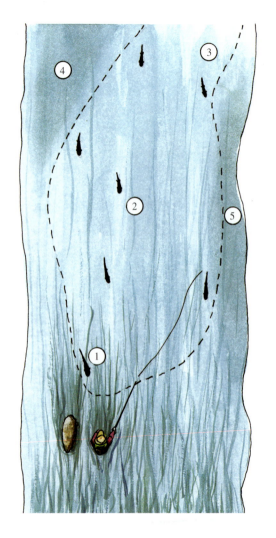

F<small>LY</small> F<small>ISHING FOR</small> S<small>TEELHEAD</small>

The river's course itself can help you read steelhead water. Look for inside bends in the river—those place where the streambed curves to the left or right, creating a pocket of soft water along the inside of the bend. Steelhead find comfortable holding water where the river wraps around a corner. Add a few boulders or depressions, and so much the better. Don't ignore the outside bends, however, as they too can offer good holding water, often close to the bank.

Study the river's surface, looking for smooth glides and choppy runs. Classic pools are easy to recognize, but smaller runs often prove equally productive and in many places escape the notice of most anglers. Even on familiar rivers, look for new runs and chutes and single-fish lies that may have escaped your attention in the past. When you recognize potential steelhead water, whether a large pool or tiny slot, make at least a few casts each time you visit the spot. Eventually you'll either hook a fish there or you'll decide the fish don't hold in that place. Regardless, the best way to learn new water is to wade and fish your way through.

In this run, the middle of the river offers the best holding water (1 and 2), and the angler is best served by casting into the deep water along the far bank so that the fly swings from deep water to shallower water through the middle of the river. At the downstream end of the pool, however, the productive slot swings to the far side (3), so anglers must make a long cast from the near side, or fish the end of the run from the other bank. Area (4) is deep enough to hold steelhead, but too slow. Conversely, the slot along the far bank (5) runs at the appropriate speed, but at eight feet it is too deep to be generally productive.

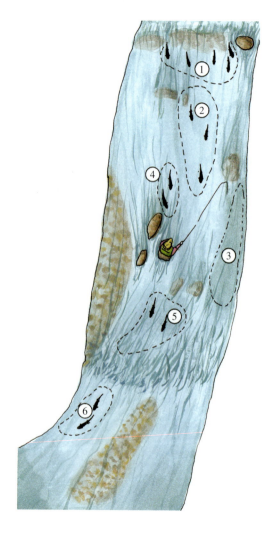

FLY FISHING FOR STEELHEAD

This complex pool offers lots of prime holding water that might potentially hold steelhead. However, the fish show decided preferences for certain areas. If just two or three fish occupy the pool, they invariably hold in area (1) immediately in front of the submerged ledge rock above a six-foot waterfall, and in area (2) in the middle of the pool, where the water is about five feet deep and flowing at the perfect pace. If the pool is loaded with steelhead, they occupy those two prime spots, along with the less desirable slots further upstream at the head of the pool (4 and 5), and sometimes in the glassy glide above the riffle (6). The area marked (3) often holds spring chinook salmon in June, but seldom holds steelhead.

A glassy tail-out—ideal steelhead water—spills over into a rapids.

For many years I've fished a spot I call the "50-Percent Hole" on a nearby river. I walk down to the head of this smooth glide and admire its perfect, fishy arrangement: A cobblestone bar drops off quite suddenly from the near bank, creating a fifty-foot chute bordered on the outside by the main current. The glassy surface is nowhere flat, but nor is it broken—perfect current speed, perfect location, four feet deep, and myriad large rocks mixed with the cobble. Ideal holding water, or so it appears. I've never hooked a fish there, yet I fish that slot every time. Looks great to me, but apparently not to the steelhead. Despite the futility, I persist in believing that some day I'll hook a fish in that run; probably I am wrong.

However, should the enterprising angler study the entire river here, he or she notices a gravel bar at midriver that slopes downstream into a perfect little steelhead pool along the far bank. To fish this quietly productive pool, one must first wade across the 50-Percent Hole, which I named because about half the time I successfully wade across and about half the time I end up swimming out at the bottom end.

Kamikaze wading notwithstanding, steelhead anglers must persist in fishing new runs and pools, for experience is the best teacher: The more fish you hook from numerous pools and runs, the more you understand about steelhead water. As your experience mounts, you learn what to look for and you soon begin to recognize certain patterns that help you ferret out steelhead on many different rivers. For the observant angler, each hookup offers a chance to learn something

A broad cobblestone steelhead pool.

new—something about reading a river for steelhead and something that can be filed away and applied to new rivers in the future.

As you fish new waters, do so unhurriedly. Make a study of the water and train yourself to recognize the characteristics that make good fly water and good steelhead holding water. Look for peculiarities unique to each pool or to each river. On many rivers, for example, winter steelhead hold in surprisingly shallow, nearshore water. Yet many anglers wade out too deep and forget to swing the fly through the two-foot-deep flows near shore. In fact, the higher the water, the more likely you are to find winter fish holding close to the banks.

Conversely, summer steelhead often take up stations in skinny, shallow tail-outs. Sometimes they act spooky

Perfect speed and perfect depth make for perfect steelhead water.

The author begins fishing at the head of a nice pool.

and skittish under such conditions and other times they seem unafraid, even unaware of any commotion around them. Most anglers prefer the skittish fish— they usually prove to be better chasers than the dour fish whose sole interest seems to be hanging out fanning their tails in the current.

Dour fish are especially common during the warm periods of late summer, when they often seek refuge in deep pools. These steelhead are especially unpredictable, especially if they are schooled together. Summer steelhead often pod up, forming schools, in staging pools below their eventual spawning destinations. On some waters, especially small rivers, good ethics dictate that we leave these staging fish to their own devices. They are vulnerable and have reached the furthest point in their migration until winter rains make the spawning tributaries accessible.

For that matter, steelhead anglers must learn to recognize spawning fish, which should be considered off limits under all circumstances. Winter steelhead typically spawn on gravel bars and gravelly tail-outs in the main river channel and its major tributaries. Being dark by spawning time, they are easy to spot in shallow water, as are their redds, which appear as patches of lighter color against the darker river bottom.

KNOW YOUR RIVER

Intimate knowledge of a river gives any steelheader the advantage over the angler who visits but rarely. The locals know the best fly water and the most consistently productive pools and runs. They know when to fish particular places and where to fish under each different set of weather and water conditions.

A conversation with my fishing partner one August day exemplifies the home-field edge: "Where should I meet you?" Forrest asked.

I pondered that for a moment and then suggested, "I'll fish Lower Bend first this afternoon because the sun will be behind the fish by four, and that'll put me down around the corner below the Rail Hole when the sun gets low enough to give me a good chance there.

"So how about we meet at the park and we can fish the confluence just about the time the sun hides behind those big fir trees," I concluded. Forrest nodded his agreement and we never gave it another thought—until now. That was typical local knowledge playing in our favor.

Some of us just rely on memory—a ploy likely to cost us in our waning years—while other anglers keep logs and notes about their rivers. Either way, keep tabs on such gems of information. Steelhead, after all, are creatures of habit. Figure out where and when they are likely to chase a fly in any given river and you've won at least half the battle.

If you're new to a river, open your eyes and your ears. Many a time I've driven up along a new river, watching for water that might offer shade during the afternoon or might yield a chance for dry-fly action. I always look for little seams and runs between the known pools—places that might yield a fish for the angler who takes the time to make a few casts.

Listen to other anglers talk about the river and ask a prudent question here and there. Certainly most steelhead fly anglers consider it bad form to ask specifically for advice on what pools to fish, unless such pools are of the super-famous variety. In other words, rather than asking an angler for directions to his favorite pool, try asking him in what kind of water the fish have been holding, what time of day has been most productive for him, or what he'd recommend in terms of flies for his river. Such harmless and inoffensive inquiries often lead to detailed answers, offers to share an evening fishing, and even lasting angling friendships.

THE STEELHEADER'S INSTINCT

The bad news first: You can't develop a steelheader's instincts overnight. Instead, you have to fish and fish a lot. That's the good news. This is a learn-on-the-job game. Steelheading teaches you to cast and to control line, to wade and to read water. The more you fish for steelhead, the better you get at fishing for steelhead. Each hookup teaches you something about reading water and presenting a fly.

Like most steelheaders, I fish my favorite rivers so regularly that I have learned many of the most likely places to expect a hookup. I'm not surprised when I hook a fish from certain specific holding areas in my favorite pools. Likewise, when I fish rivers and pools new to me, I expect to find fish in certain places. Some places just look too perfect not to hold fish, although

Not really a pool, this type of water is known as a run.

After negotiating waterfalls and heavy rapids, steelhead often hold in the first smooth water immediately above.

Steelhead often occupy the soft, deep edges along rapids like these.

the steelhead don't always agree. That's one reason I learn from each hookup: Some fish confirm that I read the water correctly and fished the pool effectively.

Other steelhead, meanwhile, come as more of a surprise, teaching me that I must tirelessly study the nature of the rivers and of the steelhead living therein. Instincts tell me to stop and throw a cast or two over a run or slot I may have overlooked in seasons past. Sometimes I'm pleasantly surprised; other times I'll fish that place a dozen times in a season before I'm convinced of the futility in persisting further. Either way, my steelheading instincts are derived from time spent on the water.

Naturally, I take satisfaction in knowing my instincts were correct and that I read the water well and earned a fish through proper presentation. Still, perfect presentation does not assure success in this game, for steelhead must first occupy the pool and then be willing to bite. On the big western rivers, anglers must simply assume that steelhead occupy each pool. Then we just cover as much water as possible in search of a willing fish. Indeed, the veteran steelhead angler, accomplished at the art of instinctive presentation, measures his success not by the number of hookups but instead by how well he fished.

9

WADING AND WADING GEAR

"A river of big round rocks is the best wading school I know. A man who can keep his feet in it should be safe anywhere."
—Roderick Haig-Brown, 1951

BOOTS AND WADERS

Big, muscular Northwest steelhead rivers demand competent wading skills and equipment. Foremost among the latter are traction devices on your wading boots. Such implements range from cleats or studs built into the soles of the boots to cleated sandals strapped onto the wading boots. In whatever form they take, studs or cleats aid immeasurably in providing secure footing in large, swift, slippery steelhead waters.

Over the years I have owned and worn just about every type of traction device available, from simple sheet metal screws twisted into the soles of my boots to cleated sandals. They all work, but not all equally. Studded sandals provide good traction on most river bottoms right up until the tips get worn off the studs in the toes and heels, after which they become hazardous, especially on rounded rocks. The latest such sandals come with replaceable cleats.

Another sandal-type product features a series of aluminum bars set in rows and attached to a rubber upper that fits over the wading boot. These have excellent traction (except on those pesky polished round rocks

149

With good steelhead water along the bank, this angler opts to wade conservatively.

along the bank), but in my experience they tend to roll to the sides because the bars aren't quite wide enough. Nonetheless, once you get used to them, they offer that extra security needed to negotiate swift runs safely.

The best of the bunch, in my opinion, are the felt-soled and studded wading boots that feature either carbide- or porcelain-tipped steel studs built into the felt. The Orvis studded boots fit in this category and offer superb traction on virtually all surfaces. They improve with use as the felt wears away, exposing more of the stud. Meanwhile, the felt soles provide good traction on the aforementioned rounded, dry rocks along the banks, which you must often traverse while walking along the rivers.

In fact, of all the surfaces you are likely to encounter on western steelhead rivers, the most hazardous are those rounded, stream-worn cobbles and boulders littering the banks of many rivers. Harmless enough while you fish through the runs with your cleats gripping their wet surfaces fairly well, such rocks usually get you while you're hustling along the banks between

Two steelheaders use the buddy system to make a tricky wade.

On some rivers, certain pools require station-to-station fishing.

pools. A generous outpouring of luck remains the sole reason I've not broken several bones taking falls on the dry, rounded rocks. Only the aforementioned steel studs grip these shoreline cobbles with any degree of integrity. All other varieties of cleats make the problem worse and contribute—at least in my experience—to your chances of losing your footing.

Felt soles with no cleats provide a good grip on dry cobble, but choose them only for small water where you will spend more time walking on the bank than wading in the river. In the heat of summer, when water temperatures allow for it, some anglers opt for cleated wading sandals or boots worn over heavy socks and matched with a pair of lightweight pants or shorts designed for saltwater flats fishing.

152

I always prefer waders, though. They may get a little cumbersome during the middle of a hot day, but come dusk I'm always glad for the dry comfort. Most steelheaders wear breathable, lightweight waders, adding the appropriate degree of layered clothing underneath. Neoprene waders, with their excellent insulating qualities, still enjoy popularity during the winter season on many waters.

No matter what waders you choose, dress warmly—many western steelhead rivers run plenty cold even during the summer. My home river, for example, typically ranges from the high 40s to the low 50s even in midsummer. And cinch up the wading belt: If you take a spill, the belt prevents water from providing an unwelcome icing and also prevents swift currents from

To fish the midriver seam, this angler must wade aggressively.

Wading big water.

FLY FISHING FOR STEELHEAD

ballooning your waders and pushing you downstream more forcefully.

Wading Safely

Two factors determine how to wade a particular pool or run. The first is the strategic consideration and the second concerns safety. As discussed in Chapter 4, a steep angle of presentation gives you the best ability to control the speed and depth of the swinging fly, so sometimes the best casting station requires fairly aggressive wading. Other times you may want to ford the river to gain access to pools or runs best fished from the far bank.

Invariably, if you wade these rivers even somewhat aggressively you'll take a spill once in a while. On some rivers—the North Umpqua and the lower Deschutes, to name two prime examples—I've often considered wading out to thigh-deep water and sitting down in the river just to get it over with! So treacherous are some reaches on these rivers that a dunking is practically a foregone conclusion, so why wait for it to sneak up on you? Seriously, though, big western steelhead rivers demand competent wading skills.

Most wading mishaps I've seen resulted from fighting the current rather than working with it. An angler wades into too swift a current, begins to lose the battle for secure footing, panics just a little, and turns toward shore intent on making a beeline into easier water. In doing so the angler is fighting the river and often ends up with waders full of cold water.

Next time you find yourself in such a situation, try this: First, don't panic. Second, aim yourself slightly *downstream* and shoreward. Third, take long strides in that direction. You'll be surprised at how easily you can extricate yourself from a tough piece of river simply by going with the current.

Employ the same tactic when you ford a large river. Start well upstream from the point where you plan to gain the opposite bank. Then simply wade down and across, using the current to your advantage instead of fighting the river. If the flow gets too strong to cross safely, just turn back to your side of the river and angle downstream back to the near bank. Obviously, if some sort of obstacle—rapids, waterfall, deep pool, deep log-

Jennifer Byers wades to the perfect casting position for the head of this pool.

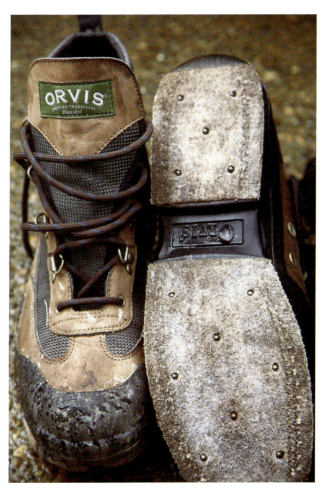

Cleated boots.

jam—lies below your path, you should consider fording the river elsewhere, especially on unfamiliar water.

On the other hand, if you are not comfortable fording broad, swift rivers, consider the conservative route of never wading across any flow that you can't successfully negotiate by going *upstream* and across. Any flow that can be forded in an upstream direction will prove unproblematic should you need reverse directions and go back downstream.

In any event, while long, down-and-across strides will usually get you across a stretch of swift, deep water, what happens if you lose your balance or accidentally wade in over your head? Obviously you'll be swimming or drifting, but the same rule applies: Don't fight the current. In slow water you can swim down and across to the shallows. In fast water, however, turn on your back with your feet downstream and steer yourself shoreward in that position.

In short, if you wade large rivers, always try to use the current to your advantage, both in crossing the stream and in recovering from an ill-fated wade or stumble. Fighting the current usually gets you in more difficulty.

10

ETIQUETTE AND ETHICS

"In other words, he is under at least a moral obligation to understand what makes his sport and why."

—Roderick Haig-Brown, 1947

In the Pacific Northwest, steelhead fly angling carries with it a particular and specific code of behavior largely borrowed from Atlantic salmon traditions. The hard and fast rules always apply to waters occupied by more than one angler, and when strictly followed by everyone involved they create a congenial atmosphere steeped in camaraderie.

When you fish through a pool or run, begin at the upstream end and move downstream at a pace of about two steps after you fish out each cast. In this manner, anglers rotate through the pool, each person beginning at the head of the productive water. When you arrive at a pool already occupied by other steelhead anglers, under no circumstances should you step in downstream of them, even if the pool stretches for hundreds of yards. Instead, walk up to the head of the pool and begin there, behind (upstream from) the anglers already fishing the water.

Better still, walk within speaking distance—never shouting distance—of the angler highest in the pool

Three anglers work down through a pool.

and ask permission to start in upstream of him or her. Good manners dictate that he or she invite you to go on up and start in at the top. Likewise the other angler should thank you for asking, for strictly speaking you needn't have done so. Still, I follow this practice wherever practical and have enjoyed meeting some wonderful people simply because I took the time to seek permission to fish behind them.

When you gain a casting position at the head of the pool, give the angler below at least a hundred feet of space, more on big water. The other anglers, like you, are obliged to keep moving downstream at a goodly pace of about two steps between casts. If a fish shows for your fly, no one will begrudge you a second or even third cast from that same station—even a fly change, done with all due haste, is generally considered allowable under such conditions, but not repeated fly changes with no additional response from the fish in question.

If you hook and play a steelhead, you forfeit your place in the run, and good manners dictate that you walk back up to the head of the pool and begin anew rather than regain your previous position below other anglers. Likewise, if an angler above you hooks a fish, give that person all the room required to wage the battle. If you step out of the water to yield to another angler's hooked and running fish, by all means begin fishing where you left off once the fish has been controlled.

Should your fly hang up on the bottom—a common occurrence whenever sinking lines are employed—never wade out deep to free the fly, because doing so may disturb the fish and spoil the chances of anglers fishing through behind you. If you can't free the fly from where you stand, move downstream and free it from below or off to one side. Then begin fishing again from that spot. Otherwise, just break off the fly—flies are easily replaced, but breaches in etiquette are not easily forgiven.

Each pool or run ends at the lowermost extent of its good holding water, the terminus being the head of the ensuing rapids, riffles, falls, narrows, or other such defining feature. You are free to fish the first good water below any such demarcation in the river's flow, because such obstacles divide one pool from the next. Anglers busy fishing the pool above enjoy no claim to the pool downstream.

Recently I enjoyed a typical exchange of good manners while fishing a pool on the Deschutes. Under encroaching dusk I had fished through the first dozen casts of the run when two other anglers greeted me from the bank. "Do you mind if we start in above you after a bit?" inquired one fellow.

"By all means," I said, "and thanks for asking."

Then I realized that only one of the other men would enjoy any amount of fishable light. I was just twenty yards into the pool, and the fading light would run out before both of the other anglers could wait for the appropriate spacing between the three of us. I reeled up, sought them out on the bank, and explained my take on the situation. "How about we divide the run into thirds," I suggested. "I'll go fish the tail-out and you two can take the middle and the head of the pool."

They were thrilled with the suggestion and appreciative of my good manners. As if the steelhead gods were properly appeased, each of us hooked a fish that evening, and for one fellow it was his first fly-caught steelhead and his inaugural experience with proper fly-angling etiquette.

Steelhead fly-fishing etiquette gets skewed on rivers also occupied by anglers using other methods. Many experienced spin fishers pursue a similar strategy of fishing downstream through the pools, but bait casters and those using drift gear often remain stationary or move about at random. Weigh each encounter on its own merits. If a stationary angler occupies the pool, either seek other water or, if space permits, ask if you can fish the water above him or below him. Don't be

particularly offended if a gear angler steps in downstream of you—he or she likely knows nothing of fly-
fishing etiquette and certainly need not abide by it.
With luck, both parties can agree on common courtesy
astream, but gear anglers generally need less space and
in many places they crowd quite close together.

Trout anglers present another issue on many rivers.
In general, I think steelhead fly anglers can yield
ground to trout fly fishers who, like gear anglers, may
know nothing of steelheading etiquette. The trout angler, fishing carefully and slowly upstream, isn't likely
to disturb steelhead, but a steelhead angler wading aggressively down through the run can very easily put
down the trout. So let the trout fishers enjoy their sport
first. Fish your way around them, or wait until they
finish. When in doubt, just ask.

In any event, you can hardly expect gear anglers or
trout fly fishers to know or abide by the rules of steelhead etiquette. But all parties can certainly agree on
good manners based on mutual respect and common
sense. Conversely, you have every right to expect fellow steelhead fly anglers to behave according to the
rules set forth above, and they should expect the same
of you.

ETHICS

While steelheading etiquette codifies our behavior
toward one another on the water, ethics define our re-
sponsibilities as stewards of the fish, their rivers, and
the history and traditions of our sport. Moreover,

The author with a beautiful native steelhead.

ethics define the parameters by which we define fair sport, or fair chase as it were.

Compared to other methods, fly fishing for steelhead requires a greater investment of time and dedication, because the necessary skills are more difficult to master. Any skilled fly angler can quickly learn to handle the spinning or casting rod as if born to it. But a gear angler, like all of us, requires good instruction and then ample sustained practice to cast ninety feet of line while standing waist deep in a swift river.

So in choosing to fly-fish for steelhead we are choosing to invest a great deal of ourselves for the satisfaction of defining fair chase by the highest standards. It is the way we play the game that counts, and we affirm as much when we decide to take up the sport.

Roderick Haig-Brown, the great author and angler who lived for many years in British Columbia, wrote at length of the angler's ethics in his masterful 1947 work entitled *The Western Angler*. He wrote: "The real fly fisherman does not simply go out fishing. He goes out to catch fish by one particular method, the use of the artificial fly, unweighted, unencumbered . . . to use any of these would be to fail in his object every bit as completely as though he had worked all day with the artificial fly and caught nothing; and he would, in addition, have deprived himself of the pleasure of a day of casting and working his fly."

Contemporary anglers sometimes pursue steelhead with methods that only superficially resemble fly fishing. On many waters, such methods might be perfectly acceptable. Indeed, indicator fishing, split shot, slinkies, and heavily weighted flies that barely qualify as flies all have their niches in the collective arsenal of steelhead angling, but their use must be guided by the highest sporting ethics. Some tactics remain entirely inappropriate on steelhead rivers or sections thereof steeped in fly-angling lore or reserved exclusively for fly fishing.

On some waters—Oregon's North Umpqua River for example—regulations help define the parameters of fair chase. But steelhead fly anglers must often decide for themselves what constitutes a fair and sporting approach to their chosen pursuit. In central Idaho's Stanley Basin, anglers converge on the upper Salmon River during March and April to pursue steelhead that are on or near their spawning grounds. That many of these steelhead are of hatchery origin is beside the point—but often the justification for fishing to them. Whether wild or from a hatchery, these remarkable steelhead have completed a nine-hundred-mile journey. They are summer-run fish and great sport on the

They command our respect.

Snake and Lower Salmon during autumn. But in spring they are well past their prime, and good ethics dictate that they have earned the right to be left alone.

So ethical questions concern not only angling methods but also the seasons or times when each run of steelhead remains the fair and proper subject of our angling efforts. Frequently we must create parameters of fair chase that go beyond those mandated by official regulations.

As you ponder the question of ethics, remember always that the classic methods of fly angling for steelhead are inarguably unique: We are asking the steelhead to leave his lair and chase our fly; we are asking him to come to us. With every other fishing method we are taking our offering to him rather than bringing him to us. The difference is paramount to everything that makes this fish so grand and fly angling for him so rewarding.

11

THE GREAT STEELHEAD RIVERS

"When the two—rivers and steelhead—unite, you have the most exciting fishing on earth."
—Art Lingren, 1994

The great steelhead rivers earned their lofty reputations over the course of many decades. Some, like Oregon's North Umpqua, have drawn fly anglers for generations, while others have earned their fame more recently. The best of them offer far more than a chance to hook steelhead on a fly—they promise an experience unlike anything else in angling. The greatest steelhead rivers allow anglers the chance to immerse themselves in local fly-fishing lore and to enjoy the quiet company of other wandering souls whose passion for steelhead and the rivers they run permeates their lives and fuels their dreams.

Yet for every famous steelhead river, at least a dozen lesser-known flows offer fishable runs of summer and or winter fish. Some of these remain hidden little gems garnering little publicity, while others attract attention from the gear-fishing community but not from fly fishers. In either case, exploration-minded anglers often find fishing on these rivers that rivals anything offered by the famous waters.

The list below features brief descriptions of the most renowned steelhead rivers—waters of long-standing fame in fly-angling circles. These days, some of the once-great rivers offer steelhead runs and fishing opportunities that can hardly compare to those of days long gone. Yet even with comparatively marginal fishing, some of these waters remain important in the history of steelhead fly angling. What follows is a brief catalog of the great steelhead rivers. For more complete details on these waters, consult the reference materials listed in the next chapter.

KALAMA RIVER, WASHINGTON

Just thirty minutes north of Portland/Vancouver flows one of Washington's most revered steelhead rivers, the Kalama, whose fly-only section serves as a haven for both wild steelhead and the catch-and-release anglers pursuing them. Both wild and hatchery steelhead enter the Kalama every month of the year, with the winter run peaking from January through March. The bulk of the summer fish arrive during June and July, but good fishing continues through September.

This easily accessible river intersects Interstate 5 just east of the Kalama's mouth on the Columbia. From I-5, Kalama River Road follows closely along the river, eventually yielding to a gravel road that runs above the fly-only reach—called the "Holy Water"— much of which requires a bit of legwork to hike down into the shallow, timbered canyon. The fly-only section fishes best between July and September and includes lots of good dry-fly water, where anglers often cast skaters to sighted fish.

The Kalama River.

During summer and fall, the Kalama is small water, easily covered with a single-handed rod and easily forded just about anywhere. The winter season, not nearly so popular with fly anglers, reveals a fairly swift river that swells quickly after heavy rains and drops back into shape rapidly when the weather improves. The river boasts one famous fly bearing its name: Decades ago, Mooch Abrams devised his Kalama

Special, which features a yellow body, palmered grizzly hackle, and white wing.

NORTH FORK STILLAGUAMISH RIVER, WASHINGTON

Though hardly the wild steelhead factory it was before rampant timber harvest devastated Deer Creek, its major tributary, the North Fork Stillaguamish—or "Stilly"—remains hallowed ground in angling circles. This river once hosted an annual pilgrimage of the sport's greatest pioneers, all of them gathering near Deer Creek when the Stilly's summer fish arrived. Among them were George and Ken McLeod, inventors of the Purple Peril and Skykomish Sunrise patterns, along with Walt Johnson, the legendary "Sasquatch of the Stilly," so named for his ability to disappear into the backwoods along the river when "city" anglers tried to learn the river by following him from a distance.

Today the Stilly continues to offer both summer and winter steelhead, with the summer and autumn fishing being especially popular with fly anglers who enjoy a fly-only season on the river's prime reach. Few summer fish reach double digits—most range from four to eight pounds. Unlike some of northern Washington's other steelhead streams, the Stilly offers a stable streambed that varies little from year to year. This small river's most famous pools fish the same from year to year. The town of Arlington is the jumping-off point for anglers headed to the Stilly. From I-5 and

The North Fork Stillaguamish River.

Arlington, State Route 503 heads east along the North Fork.

SKAGIT/SAUK RIVERS, WASHINGTON

With its traditional catch-and-release season in late winter, northwest Washington's Skagit River reigns among the Pacific Northwest's most popular destinations for hard-core steelhead fly anglers. The attraction—besides the beautiful Skagit Valley itself—is the river's run of big, native winter steelhead. Most exceed ten pounds and many reach fourteen pounds. Each season, a few lucky fly anglers tangle with twenty-pounders. Nobody catches lots of these fish: The Skagit is a huge river during winter and spring, when its broad meanders reach out across expansive gravel bars.

The river runs a wide, low-gradient course through the prime water below the hamlet of Marblemount, and the uninitiated often feel a slight sense of intimidation on first witnessing the Skagit's size and shape. A casual glance leaves one wondering just where to cast the fly, but a closer inspection reveals subtle current seams and surface characteristics intimating those

The Sauk River.

The Skagit River.

FLY FISHING FOR STEELHEAD

places ideal for holding steelhead. The best and most popular water stretches from Marblemount down to the town of Concrete, a reach paralleled on the north bank by State Route 20. The highway offers ready bank access in a few places, but boaters enjoy the advantage.

About halfway through this stretch, the Sauk River flows into the Skagit from the south. In contrast to the Skagit, the smaller Sauk runs a steeper course, her flows usually tinged green from winter rains or gray from glacial till—the river emanates from the ice fields of Glacier Peak. Often the Sauk runs high and off-color, dirtying the Skagit below the confluence, while the upper drift on the Skagit runs quite clear. The Skagit's better water quality derives both from its tailwater source and from the fact that most of its drainage lies within North Cascades National Park, whose forest tracts have not suffered the rampant timber harvest visited upon the slopes of the Sauk drainage.

Hoh, Sol Duc, and Bogachiel rivers, Washington

Flowing gracefully through the impossibly lush evergreen forests of Washington's Olympic Peninsula, the Hoh, Sol Duc, and Bogachiel rivers inarguably define the traditions of winter steelhead fly fishing. Each of these three rivers presents a different personality. The Sol Duc flows ruggedly over boulder-strewn runs while her sister river, the beautiful "Bogy" reveals a

The Hoh River.

gentler demeanor. Both rivers, along with the Calawah, converge to form the Quillayute River. Unlike the Quillayute system just to the north, the famous Hoh River feeds directly off the glaciers of the Olympic Range, so her flows frequently run tinged with gray-green.

The Hoh, characterized by broad gravel bars and braided channels, flows through Olympic National Park on its westward journey. Its prime steelhead stretch begins several miles inside the park boundary and extends about twenty miles down to the Highway 101 bridge. Bank access is limited (but available in places), so drift boats are the rule. Because of its glacial sources, the Hoh is a good choice during bouts of cold, dry weather—the glacial till subsides and the water clears appreciably.

Of the three rivers, the Hoh is the best for swinging classic flies on fast-sinking lines because the cobble riverbed is quite clean and free of obstructions. The Bogy and the Sol Duc offer prime pools for swung flies, but also feature lots of boulder-studded pocket

The Sol Duc River.

water, where many anglers opt for weighted flies and sink-tip lines. The Sol Duc offers the best bank access of the three rivers, with Highway 101 paralleling the river for many miles. Also, of the three rivers, the Sol Duc offers the best run of summer steelhead between June and October.

These waters will forever be known as the birthplace of the steelhead Spey fly, for it was here that the late Syd Glasso created his Orange Heron and other remarkable patterns. He married steelhead colors with the old Spey fly designs to launch a new era in steelhead fly tying. Today—half a century later—the Glasso legacy is stronger than ever, evident in the countless Spey-style designs used by anglers throughout the Pacific Northwest.

GRANDE RONDE RIVER, WASHINGTON

Carving out a steep, dramatic canyon on its rapid descent from the remote mountains of northeastern Oregon, the Grande Ronde finally reaches the Snake River about an hour south of Clarkston, Washington at Heller Bar. From the tiny town of Troy, eight miles inside Oregon, the Grande Ronde twists and turns and bends its way through arid steeps, offering many miles of perfect fly water easily covered with the classic down-and-across swing. The river's relatively steep gradient makes its steelhead pools and runs perfectly discernible.

The summer-run steelhead for which the "Ronde" is famous travel about four hundred and fifty miles from

The Grande Ronde River.

the sea, first negotiating the gauntlet of dams on the Columbia and Snake rivers. These days, the precious few wild Grande Ronde steelhead join ranks with lots of hatchery-produced fish. Wild or not, Grande Ronde fish rank among the best dry-fly steelhead anywhere: So long as autumn water temperatures remain above 50 degrees or so, these fish behave aggressively and will move considerable distances to explode on a skater or slam a wet fly. Though most weigh just six to nine pounds, they pack a substantial punch, often running deep into the backing.

Most years, cooling water draws steelhead into the lower reaches of the Grande Ronde by mid-September. The first two miles above the Snake River are paralleled by road. Additional drive-in access awaits well upstream, from the bridge at Boggan's Oasis up to Troy as well as from the rugged road to Shumaker's, downstream from Boggan's. The Grande Ronde is easy to float, save for the nasty section called The Narrows on the lower drift, where the river funnels between rock banks. Only experienced oarsmen should float the lower drift, which requires at least two days. Troy to Boggan's and Boggan's to Shumaker's make easy one-day floats.

ROGUE RIVER, OREGON

Oregon's most southerly run of summer steelhead ascends the lengthy and legendary Rogue River, most of them reaching the Middle and Upper Rogue during September and October. The run is comprised largely of steelhead exhibiting the half-pounder life history. (See Chapter 1.) These fish include the true half-pounders that range from twelve to sixteen inches, as well as the repeat-run half-pounders—adult fish of seventeen to twenty-four inches. A small contingent of the run consists of the typical one- and two-salt

The Rogue River.

summer fish common further north. These adults range from eight to fourteen pounds.

The Rogue drains a vast watershed and includes several significant tributaries. In addition to its summer-run fish, the Rogue system boasts a sizable run of winter steelhead between late December and April. The Rogue's massive wintertime presence limits the fly-angling opportunities, but fly anglers enjoy consistent success on the Applegate and Illinois Rivers, two of the main feeder streams.

Three fairly distinct reaches of the lengthy Rogue offer their own unique characteristics. The lower river, which runs for many miles through a roadless wilderness canyon, begins at Grave Creek and extends downstream to the mouth. The roadless section, from Grave Creek to the hamlet of Agness, features many rugged, dangerous rapids of long-standing repute with whitewater enthusiasts. Here the Rogue hurls its way through a precipitous, timbered canyon. The Lower Rogue enjoys the services of several famous riverside lodges that anglers reach by boat.

From Grave Creek upstream to the Grants Pass area, the river takes the name Middle Rogue. The lower end of the Middle Rogue features stunning forested slopes clad in oaks and conifers and plunges down to a scenic mix of broad, glassy tail-outs, extensive rapids, and deep, ledge-bound and bubble-shot pools. The Middle Rogue is the likely birthplace of the tactic of "pulling" flies: The oarsman instructs the angler to cast the fly downstream from the back of a drift boat. Then the oarsman simultaneously rows against the current, forcing the boat to slip downstream slower than current speed, and steers the boat from side to side to swing the fly though the currents. Decades old, this tactic allowed guides to successfully fish clients with limited ability in waters that are largely unwadable.

Upstream from Grants Pass, above two impoundments and below a third, flows the Upper Rogue, which offers a fly-only fishery during the fall when small adult steelhead return in substantial numbers. These sixteen- to twenty-four-inch fish, mostly of hatchery origin, respond to both traditional steelheading tactics and also to methods more commonly used for trout. Indeed, most local anglers fish for them using nymph-and-indicator rigs. The town of Shady Cove is the hub of activity on this portion of the river.

NORTH UMPQUA RIVER, OREGON

Steeped in fly-angling lore and tradition, the North Umpqua serves simultaneously as both the most beautiful steelhead river and the most demanding. Boasting a thirty-mile fly-only section, the North Umpqua carves out a steep, forested canyon and flows over ancient bedrock on its oft-tumultuous westward run. The landscape's steep, rock-bound gradient creates a river characterized by short, swift rapids interspersed with gentle, glassy pools and deep, gliding runs.

Of the North Umpqua's unique nature, author Clark C. Van Fleet once wrote: "The roar of its mighty voice fills the canyon from source to junction as it tumbles down the rough, boulder-strewn cleft carved by its journey. A mile of fishing along its banks is a very real test of endurance as you snake your way over the folds in the bedrock, scramble onto jagged reefs and cross huge piles of rubble."

Like most North Umpqua visitors, Van Fleet was duly impressed by the river's intimidating physical character. On this fabled river, the problem lies not so much in determining where the steelhead are likely to hold, but in devising a ploy to properly present a fly to them on the many complex, physically demanding pools. Van Fleet realized, as North Umpqua addicts do today, that a "successful analysis of the North Umpqua, and you will qualify anywhere steelhead are taken."

Summer steelhead, of both native and hatchery origin, arrive between June and October, with the bulk of

The North Umpqua River.

the fishing pressure occurring in August and September. The summer fish typically range from four to ten pounds with enough really big fish around to keep you on your toes. They are strong, fast, high-spirited fish and the best of them use the steep river to their advantage: The term "went over" originated here, and refers to hooked steelhead that run downstream out of the pool and over the next rapids, almost always freeing themselves from the hook in the process. "He went over," is a simple descriptive sentence understood by all North Umpqua regulars.

The North Umpqua's winter-run steelhead arrive between January and late March. All are natives and a few exceed twenty pounds. Lots of them range from eight to twelve pounds. Local anglers enjoy a huge advantage during the winter season because the river level fluctuates so wildly and so rapidly in reaction to rainfall and snowmelt.

Highway 138 departs I-5 at Roseburg and heads east, reaching the fly water upstream from the little community of Idelyld. About halfway through the fly water flows the river's most famous reach, the Camp Water. On this scenic bend in the river, anglers enjoy the privilege of fishing over hallowed pools like Sawtooth, Station, The Boat Pool, Kitchen, The Gordon Pools, and the Mott Pool. Situated along the highway above the Camp Water, the famous Steamboat Inn has for decades served as a gathering place for steelhead anglers.

Happily no boats are allowed on the famous reaches of the North Umpqua's fly water. Moreover, the North

Umpqua, after an arduous battle at century's end, became the only steelhead river where regulations forbid the use of weighted flies during the summer season. As a result, the North Umpqua reverted to the gentlemanly river it had been in Van Fleet's time.

LOWER DESCHUTES RIVER, OREGON

The Lower Deschutes River runs south to north for about a hundred miles, reaching the Columbia River east of The Dalles, Oregon, an hour and a half east of Portland. This massive river offers boundless opportunities for summer-run steelhead ranging from four to twenty pounds. Typical steelhead here run from five to eight pounds with both native and hatchery fish in abundance. A few fish venture upriver as early as June, but the fishing begins in earnest during the heat of August, at least on the lower twenty-five miles of the river. By September, the fish are well distributed throughout the river, and good sport continues into November.

Deschutes River access proves tedious in many stretches, especially the twenty-five miles of roadless water from Macks Canyon to the mouth. This reach is the domain of jetboats running up from the mouth and drift boats departing from the launch at Macks Canyon. Above Macks Canyon, seventeen miles of rough gravel road parallels the east bank. Above the gravel road, eight miles of paved road follow the river to the little town of Maupin, and six more miles of gravel reach upstream to the "Locked Gate." The

The Deschutes River.

upper reaches of the river can be accessed at Warm Springs, Trout Creek, and South Junction. Drift boats reign throughout this upper half of the river, but throughout its run the Lower Deschutes requires strong skills at the oars.

Renowned for its treacherous wading, the Deschutes demands cleated boots. The water, always just slightly off color and running over dark-colored rocks, is difficult to see through. Many steelhead pools are carved from bedrock, and reefs and ledges create uneven wading. For a few steps you fish from atop a ledge, the water barely reaching your knees, only to step off into cold, neck-deep flows at the downstream end of the rock. The steelhead, however, find ample holding

A Deschutes River native.

FLY FISHING FOR STEELHEAD

water amid the ledges, boulders, and seams that abound in this broad, muscular river.

Like most storied steelhead rivers, the Deschutes offers a short list of its own well-known fly patterns. Among the most famous Deschutes flies are Doug Stewart's popular Max Canyon and Randall Kaufmann's Freight Train.

THOMPSON RIVER, BRITISH COLUMBIA

Carving a scenic course through the arid, aptly named High Country of south-central British Columbia, the Thompson River annually hosts one of the West's great autumn gatherings of steelhead fly-angling addicts. This popular river boasts a run of big summer steelhead, renowned for their aggressiveness and remarkable strength. Their two-hundred-mile migration requires these ten- to twenty-pound-plus trophies to run the powerful flows of the Fraser River and then negotiate the brutal force of the lower reaches of the Thompson.

Once through the canyons and gorges of the Thompson's lower end, these two- and three-salt fish finally arrive at British Columbia's most famous stretch of steelhead fly water. Less than fifteen miles in length, the Thompson's popular and productive reach near Spences Bridge features more than a dozen named pools of long-standing repute, including Big Horn Pool, Graveyard Run, Hotel Run, and the Grease Hole.

The Thompson's fish—several thousand of them most years—arrive during autumn, allowing anglers a brief window for fishing dry flies before the icy winds arrive, hinting at the harsh winters of the High Country. October is prime time, especially for dry flies, and the action continues until winter sets in for the season, usually during November. As water temperatures fall and steelhead become less aggressive, anglers switch to sink-tip lines to swing wet flies deeper in the flow.

A demanding river in many respects, the Thompson's broad pools often demand long-distance casting—one reason that two-handed rods now prevail on the river. In addition, the Thompson confronts anglers with difficult wading created by the river's abundance of slippery, round cobble and boulders, many of which have a maddening tendency to roll when you try to gain the advantage of perching atop them.

The angler's gathering point at Spences Bridge lies south of the town of Ashcroft and some 185 miles northeast of Vancouver via the Trans-Canada Highway. The temperate climate of coastal British Columbia yields to a more arid highland climate as you enter the 21,000-square-mile drainage of the Thompson. By the time you reach Spences Bridge, only scattered groves of stately pines guard the river's course, though dense stands of Douglas fir and larch cap the wind-carved slopes high above.

DEAN RIVER, BRITISH COLUMBIA

Truly a wilderness river, the Dean carves out a magnificent journey through the impossibly steep, snow-capped crags of the coastal mountains in B.C.'s

Cariboo-Chilcotin Coast region. The river's prime section stretches for many miles from Crag Creek to the mouth, most of it is accessible only by boat or air service. The river's steelhead arrive chrome bright and fresh from the nearby Pacific, with the peak season extending from late July through September.

Famous for its bright summer steelhead and wilderness environs, the Dean seems designated by higher powers to run a course and speed ideal for fly angling, and indeed it enjoys a fly-only season throughout the summer. Art Lingren, the prominent angling historian from Vancouver, wrote: "In Norse mythology Valhalla was the place where Odin received the souls of heroes slain in battle. Some steelhead fly-fishing aficionados believe that the Dean is where all dedicated practitioners are received by the god of steelhead fly fishing."

Drawing some of its headwaters from glacial sources in the rugged coastal mountains, the Dean often runs tinged by grayish silt. Generally the water clarity improves as the season progresses, but unseasonably hot weather or heavy rain can reduce water clarity substantially at any time. Rarely during the season does the river run gin-clear, but it can approach such a condition.

Most Dean River steelhead range from eight to ten pounds, having spent two years at sea. Three-salt fish make up about 10 percent of the run, so anglers enjoy a reasonable chance at large, double-digit fish, some of which exceed twenty pounds. Because their journey into the popular fly water spans such a short distance, these fish tend to be nickel bright and full of spirit.

The difficulty with the Dean is getting on the river. Only a handful of outfitters are licensed to guide the twenty-five miles of roadless water, and mostly they cater to longtime repeat clients. Interested parties must research the matter well ahead of time to lock in a spot with the outfitters. The river is floatable from points above the roadless reach down to the road-accessible takeouts at Grizzly Run and the Fisheries Cabin. Complete details are available in Art Lingren's *Steelhead River Journal: Dean.* (See Suggested Reading.)

Skeena Tributaries, British Columbia

One of the great tributaries of the massive Skeena River system, the Babine River is famous as the home of the world's largest steelhead. Giant summer-run fish, many weighing more than twenty pounds, ascend this medium-sized river during the fall, and each year a few fortunate anglers land fish of thirty pounds or more! The prospects for huge steelhead would pique any angler's interest, but unfortunately the Babine is terribly difficult to access, and virtually all successful fly anglers fish the river through one of a handful of lodges on the upper reaches of the river. Moreover, booking a stay on the Babine generally requires adding your name to a waiting list and then spending thousands of dollars for the privilege of fishing this coveted water.

Some bank access is available downstream from the weir at the river's source, Babine/Nilkitkwa Lake, but the best water lies below, in the next fifteen miles or so, and is inaccessible to bank anglers. Additionally, the river is unfloatable through its remote, bear-infested course—it crashes through unnavigable Class IV and V rapids about twenty miles below the lake. Such exclusivity keeps the water free of crowds, of course, but anglers need deep pockets for a crack at the Babine's remarkable trophy steelhead.

Like its neighbor the Babine, the Kispiox River hosts a run of huge summer steelhead that arrive in this Skeena tributary during autumn. Prime fishing occurs in October and lasts into November—if the weather cooperates. Inclement weather spoils the river quickly, and it takes a while to clear after heavy rains. Unlike the Babine, the Kispiox offers ready and abundant access and is easily floated in just about any kind of watercraft.

At ideal flows, the Kispiox is a beautiful steelhead stream of intermediate size, lined with cottonwoods, and ideal for fly casting. The river's broad cobble bars curl the currents into well-defined pools and runs, all with a backdrop of snow-capped highlands. Logging roads follow the river, which offers almost forty miles of prime water.

The rather diminutive Bulkley River converges with the larger Morice River near the town of Houston, British Columbia and thereafter the river goes by the name of the smaller fork. The scenic and easily floated Bulkley enjoys widespread fame for its aggressive, surface-oriented, summer-run steelhead. They pounce on skated and skittered dry flies during the prime season from late September through mid-October. Moreover, the river offers the robust steelhead typical of the Skeena system, with fourteen- to twenty-pound fish quite common.

The prime water on the Bulkley runs from Houston down to Telkwa. Broad cobblestone runs and wide pools characterize this low-gradient section of the river. Below Telkwa, the Bulkley picks up speed and is left mostly to the abundant jet boats.

The Morice River offers a personality quite different from that of its sister stream, the Bulkley. Equally scenic, the Morice flows through a narrow valley, and the river's course is subject to frequent alterations from the spring and summer runoff. Likewise, the annual high flows create dynamic braided channels replete with sweepers and boulder gardens. Such obstacles make the Morice troublesome to negotiate, so only expert oarsmen should apply. Otherwise, decent access is available via local logging roads.

SMITH RIVER, CALIFORNIA

Just a few miles from the Oregon border, the Smith River is California's last great refuge for anadromous fish, including a fine run of native winter steelhead, now supplemented by hatchery fish. No dams interrupt the Smith's emerald flows, and she remains the longest unimpounded river in the state, flowing gracefully through ancient redwood groves in her lower reaches a few miles from the Pacific.

The Smith's most popular reach begins at The Forks, where the South Fork and Middle Fork con-

The Smith River.

verge to form the main stem. Below The Forks, the Smith sneaks through Jedediah Smith State Park, home to the world's tallest trees. The redwood trees here span countless human generations, many of them having taken root centuries before Tutankhamun ruled Egypt. Within the state park, famous pools like Whitehorse Riffle and the Park Hole draw dedicated fly anglers each winter. They gather on these waters for the chance at those rare encounters with the Smith's big two- and three-salt winter steelhead. In fact, most of California's largest steelhead—including the state record twenty-seven-pound fish—have hailed from the approximately fifteen pools and runs between Highway 101 and Highway 99.

Never imperiled by the ice sheets that covered the mountains further north during the great Ice Ages, the Smith's ancient watershed remains well preserved and intact. Her riparian forests enjoy the protection afforded not only by the state park, but also by the river's status as a federally designated Wild and Scenic River. The Smith was the first watershed on which the U.S. Forest Service banned logging on steep inner gorge slopes—a timber harvest practice that decimated many steelhead spawning streams elsewhere in the state.

The forks of the Smith drain some of the state's most pristine country. Of the three branches, the South Fork Smith offers the wildest and most remote opportunities for winter steelhead. Highway 199 follows the Middle Fork. About 90 percent of the Smith's 500-square-mile drainage lies on public lands.

Of all the coastal rivers in northern California, the Smith is always the last to blow out after heavy rains and the first to clear when the weather breaks. Her natal forest—more intact than the riparian areas surrounding the other rivers—acts like a sponge, absorbing and holding rain and filtering out sediment. Consequently the Smith frequently runs remarkably clean and clear, even during the prime steelhead season from February through March.

EEL RIVER, CALIFORNIA

In large measure, the Eel River serves as a sobering reminder of how once-great California rivers have tragically fallen victim to the ravages of unchecked timber harvest and water allocation. This easily accessed river still enjoys a good run of winter steelhead, but few contemporary anglers realize what the river once offered, including pure, clean, cold flows that formed deep, inviting steelhead pools even near the river's mouth. Indeed, while a scant few steelhead return to the river during autumn, the Eel once enjoyed high repute among a who's who of legendary California steelhead fly anglers.

In his classic 1951 book *Steelhead to a Fly,* the venerable angler and author Clark C. Van Fleet wrote extensively about angling for summer steelhead on the Eel during the 1920s and 1930s. By the time he authored his book, Van Fleet felt compelled to remind readers that: "It would be misleading to give the impression that there has not been a material reduction in the numbers

The Eel River in the redwoods.

of steelhead migrating up the Eel annually compared to 30 years ago. Spawning streams have been choked with debris where timber has been removed from adjacent watersheds; irrigation and power projects have both diminished the water supply and blocked portions of the river for ingress and egress; fishing has increased a hundred fold in the past quarter century, all with their consequent effect on fish life. Yet with all these increasing hazards to overcome, this hardy sea-going rainbow still runs the river in goodly numbers."

Today, the winter steelhead fishing peaks between late December and March, although during particularly wet winters, the river blows out for the entire season, a consequence of the denuded watershed still many years away from recovery. When ideal water conditions arrive, hordes of anglers often arrive as well. In crowded conditions, fly anglers are best served by exploring the forks. Otherwise, the well-known pools from the convergence of the forks down to the mouth remain the most popular.

More than a century ago, Eel River fly anglers devised methods to fish the slow-moving pools of the lower river. They arrived at a variation on the wet fly swing in which they would quarter the cast down and across and then strip line during the swing to enliven the fly and tempt oft-dour steelhead into chasing and striking. In the early days of Eel River fame, anglers enjoyed fishing to pods or even huge schools of sea-bright steelhead resting in relatively deep, gin-clear waters. Today's water conditions rarely compare, but the "strip-tease" technique remains a staple on the lower reaches of the Eel.

KLAMATH RIVER, CALIFORNIA

Like the Eel River to the south, the Klamath River suffers mightily from a watershed degraded for decades by the commercial intrusions of humans. Indeed, even to this day the river often runs so low and warm during summer that few of the Klamath's chinook salmon enjoy any chance of surviving long enough to reproduce, and in 1999 the river was essentially dewatered, leading to a salmon kill of epic proportions.

Despite its hardships, the Klamath still offers the state's best run of half-pounders, the small, immature steelhead that also ascend Oregon's Rogue River during the fall. The Klamath half-pounder fishing begins in mid- to late September and peaks in October when water temperatures remain perfect for dry-line fishing. By November, these twelve- to sixteen-inch steelhead

A Klamath River half-pounder.

reach the upper stretches of the river accessible by Highway 96. Mixed among the half-pounders are a few small adult steelhead of three to six pounds, virtually all of which are second-year half-pounders. Between January and March the river draws a decent run of slightly larger winter steelhead.

The Klamath, whose watershed drains more than 12,000 square miles, reaches the Pacific sixty miles north of Eureka. Highway 169 follows much of the lower river, reaching Highway 96 at the confluence of the Klamath and its major tributary, the Trinity River. The long, scenic drive on Highway 96 snakes along the Klamath for many miles, often dipping close to the river and offering ready fishing access. In other places the road climbs high above the water and provides spectacular vistas.

The Trinity River is the Klamath's major tributary, arriving from the south after a long, winding journey down from the Trinity Alps. Well known for its run of winter steelhead, the Trinity offers ready roadside access and lots of fine fly water. The winter run extends from December through March.

CLEARWATER RIVER, IDAHO

Flowing broad and bold on its westward journey toward the Snake River, Idaho's Clearwater is home to the largest summer steelhead found south of the Canadian border. The river's so-called "B-run" steelhead typically spend two or three years in the ocean, where they reach double-digit weights, with twelve- to fifteen-pound fish

The Clearwater River.

being typical. These Clearwater brutes—like all Idaho steelhead—undertake the most arduous journey of any salmonids.

Upon smolting, the juvenile fish (both wild and hatchery) head downstream to the Snake, then down the Columbia. Their unlikely journey covers some six hundred miles and passes seven dams. As adults they must renegotiate the gauntlet of dams, none of which were designed and built during times when optimal fish passage was of foremost concern. Nonetheless, these remarkable Clearwater fish—like their brethren bound for other Snake River tributaries—return in sufficient numbers to create a popular fishery where fly anglers enjoy the chance to hook the fish of a lifetime.

The Clearwater draws its headwaters from the remote, forested mountains of north-central Idaho. Tributaries include the Selway and Lochsa rivers, which converge to form the main river. Joining the flow downstream, the North Fork Clearwater once hosted the world's largest population of spawning summer steelhead, but Dworshack Dam, built with no means of fish passage, doomed the run.

An autumn fishery, the Clearwater peaks during October, when the bulk of the big B-run fish arrive and when the water is still warm enough to allow for dry-line fishing. So long as warm weather and warm water persist, anglers often choose skated dry flies. The fishing continues through November. Owing to the river's width and to frequent afternoon winds, Clearwater anglers have increasingly embraced two-handed Spey rods.

Snake River, Idaho/Washington

Gushing, gin-clear mountain springs emanate from lush meadows in a mountainous, ancient volcanic caldera. The springs gather and join the outflows from a sprawling natural lake to form a beautiful, low-gradient stream bubbling through verdant lodgepole pine forests. This could be any of hundreds of Rocky Mountain headwaters, but in this case, these unassuming origins soon forge a river so substantial that it alone has allowed thousands of years of human life to thrive across vast miles of what is now southern and western Idaho and southeastern Washington.

The Snake River once hosted astounding runs of salmon and steelhead that migrated from the Pacific, all the way up the Columbia, into the Snake, and as far upriver as a set of impassable falls in south-central Idaho. Preserved only in the history books and in the traditions of some native peoples, those long-distance Snake River migrants now return only as far as the dams allow. Snake River steelhead fishing now ends with the impoundments at Hells Canyon, but what remains can be highly productive during autumn when the summer-run fish arrive.

The Snake forms Idaho's border with southeastern Washington and eastern Oregon. The most accessible and popular steelheading extends from Clarkston, Washington upstream to the good fly water below the mouth of the Grande Ronde River. The fish include both hatchery and wild steelhead destined for the Grande Ronde, Salmon, and Clearwater rivers, so most range from five to ten pounds with a few trophy-class steelhead available.

SALMON RIVER, IDAHO

Idaho's Salmon River is home to the world's long-distance champion steelhead. These remarkable summer-run fish negotiate the Columbia and Snake rivers before traveling the entire length of the Salmon across the central Idaho wilderness to reach their traditional spawning grounds in the enchanting Stanley Basin. Their unlikely journey covers some nine hundred miles and climbs almost seven thousand feet above sea level!

Like other long-distance summer steelhead, these fish overwinter in large pools until the spring thaw, at which time they push ahead on the last leg of their journey to the headwaters of the Salmon and its forks.

Between September and early November, when the fish are in prime condition, these steelhead occupy beautiful fly water on the lower river, much of which is accessible only by boat. In the eighty miles of rugged terrain from Riggins to the river's mouth, the Salmon rages through dramatic arid canyons. During good years, enough fish show up during September and October to allow for fine sport on skated dry flies until the water temperatures drop with the arrival of cold weather. Above Riggins, altitude increases quickly, and the steelhead migrate into the wilderness reaches of this undammed river. Most will overwinter in deep pools through the wilderness and along the upper Salmon. In dry, warm years, some late autumn fishing is available upstream from the wilderness boundaries.

Given their remarkable life's journey that takes them nine hundred miles to the Pacific and then nine hundred miles—and seven dams—back, these steelhead deserve a deep respect. Yet the state of Idaho and some of its fly anglers insult these fish by pursuing them on their spawning grounds during a spring season designated for just such an affront to good steelheading ethics. Having made the longest migration of any steelhead, these awe-inspiring Salmon River fish deserve unfettered respite once the fall season ends, and certainly they should be afforded such respect on their natal waters in the Stanley Basin.

12

PLANNING A STEELHEAD TRIP

"But now I had, at least, the needed stimulation. I had hooked one. From this time on I tried with tremendous zest. Everything else was neglected— gainful pursuits, meals, everything. I talked, lived, and dreamed steelhead. Nothing else was important."

—Syl MacDowell, 1948

Timing is everything in steelhead fishing. You must arrive when the fish are in the river and when water conditions are conducive to fly angling. Years ago I used to work myself into a lather awaiting the arrival of the first few thousand summer-run fish in the river near my home. Inevitably these inaugural migrants, tallied as they passed the fish windows at the falls well downstream, reached my home waters by mid-May. I would rush out the door before first light, eager to find that first willing player among the early-arriving steelhead.

Instead, I would nearly always find the river still swollen by the high flows of spring runoff in the mountains above and running too cold to offer much hope for dry-line action. I persisted in this pursuit for a few seasons and stumbled upon but a mere handful of steelhead. In the light of many years' experience I realize now that I should have exercised more patience,

Deschutes River guide Tim Doherty with a native steelhead.

for only a quarter or so of those first few thousand fish were destined for my particular tributary. Thus, perhaps five hundred steelhead occupied forty miles of river by mid-May, leaving me with little hope of finding fish so early in the season.

Of course, any steelhead angler would forgive me my persistence and enthusiasm back in those days, especially since the drive to the prime water covered but twenty miles. For the angler planning a trip to faraway waters, however, the lesson is obvious: When you travel to a steelhead river, go when the water is at its

A good guide is also a good instructor.

Discolored water required the author to switch to a sink-tip despite the low summer flows.

best and the fish most numerous. You can gather such information from myriad sources. Consult the guidebooks listed on page 214, check with fisheries departments, call local fly shops, and peruse the Internet.

Always check current regulations governing the river you intend to fish. Steelhead regulations are constantly revised and retooled. The best way to keep up to date is to check with the fish and game department.

If you are visiting a steelhead river for the first time, consider hiring an experienced guide, but make sure you and your guide share a clear understanding of what you hope to accomplish during your time on the river. If you wish to try a particular method or work

The stuff of dreams—the author battles a summer fish.

with specific tackle, be clear with your guide about such plans. Expect your guide to fish you on good water and, if needed, to help you with technique. But remember that no matter how skilled he or she may be, the guide is also at the mercy of the steelhead and their behavior. Lots of guided steelhead outings end with no fish on the line. That's just steelheading.

EPILOGUE

From the moment my cleated boots gripped the slippery cobble I enjoyed that weird "fishy" feeling. A golden-hued sunrise had ushered in this September day, a day not appreciably different from any other except that the yellow-trimmed maple leaves intimated that this would be my last day of the season on my home river. Soon the upriver dam would release its autumn flow, and I would be walking the high ridges for blue grouse and casting pretty flies across the North Umpqua's legendary pools.

But this day would end my season on the pools etched so precisely in my mind; the pools I could wade blindfolded; the pools shared with the best of friends and few others; the pools granting the memories that fuel my angling dreams.

With each September comes this day, a day when I string the rod in an unhurried, reflective mood, fondly contemplating the season now ending. Always this day is tinged with regret born of a longing for more misty summer mornings when the *swish-swish* of the fly line seems to echo out across the river in perfect harmony with the water ouzel's melodious chorus and the song sparrow's excited scoldings; more warm evenings when extravagant sunsets trace tendrils of scarlet across the summer sky.

This morning had passed pleasantly as I'd cast across three elegant pools before noon. I had not a fish to show for my efforts, a fact that weighed very little on my mind, for I had covered the water well; I had fished the pools gracefully. With steelhead, fishing well means something—these remarkable fish deserve a certain reverence earned by their rite of passage, their unique, unlikely life's journey from fresh water to seawater to fresh water once again. One might report that "the fishing is good," but I'd rather hear you say, "I fished well today."

That September morning I had fished well. Now I was simply fishing because it seemed the thing to do, the best way to enjoy the sunny afternoon warmth that would eventually surrender to that magical last hour of daylight that heralds so many connections between summer steelhead and steelhead anglers. I enjoyed each cast, watching the narrow loops jump out over the water and unfurl across the flow. I had chosen for my fly the Maxwell's Purple Matuka, that locally renowned fly devised by my fishing partner and one of only a handful of patterns to which I entrust my fortunes astream.

I two-stepped the pool and fished down into the deepening lower reach, when finally a heavy resistance snapped the line taut. The fish was well hooked. He had taken the fly in midswing and likely had the point buried deep in the hinge of his jaws. Despite the relative improbability of this midday, sun-on-the-water hookup, I was not the least surprised, even by his impressive proportions. He battled gallantly, first dredging the depths and running deep into the hole below, and then springing skyward in a series of greyhounding tailwalks. Through it all I handled him gently, but when the thrashing subsided I leaned hard into him, steering him shoreward. I would not yield ground; instead I trusted my heavy tippet and soon had a magnificent buck by the tail. Cradling the fish underwater, his head pointed upstream, I admired this remarkable creature, a two-salt summer steelhead bearing the crimson stripe of autumn. Reluctant to release the moment, I knelt down beside this powerful, magnificent seagoing rainbow, turned his head slightly, and looked into his lively eye. Then I freed him as he had freed me: My season was now over. I unhitched the fly, dried it, and clipped it back into my battle-scared Wheatley. Then I sat beside the river for a time, watching the breeze ripple the cottonwoods. I sat there until the sun dipped below the trees. Next season was half a year distant, but already the river and its steelhead beckoned my return.

SUGGESTED READING:
GREAT BOOKS ON STEELHEAD

Baughman, Michael, *A River Seen Right*, New York: Lyons & Burford, 1995.

Bradner, Enos, *Northwest Angling*, New York: A.S. Barnes & Company, 1950.

Combs, Trey, *Steelhead Fly Fishing and Flies*, Portland, OR: Salmon Trout Steelheader, 1976.

Haig-Brown, Roderick, *Fisherman's Fall*, Vancouver, B.C.: Douglas & McIntyre, 1964.

Haig-Brown, Roderick, *Fisherman's Summer*, New York: William Morrow & Company, 1959.

Haig-Brown, Roderick, *The Western Angler*, New York: William Morrow & Company, 1947.

Kreider, Claude, *Steelhead*, New York: G.P. Putnam's Sons, 1948.

MacDowell, Syl, *Western Trout*, New York: Alfred A. Knopf, 1948.

Van Fleet, Clark C., *Steelhead to a Fly*, Boston: Little, Brown and Company, 1954.

Wahl, Ralph, *One Man's Steelhead Shangri-La*, Portland, OR: Frank Amato Publications, 1989.

GUIDEBOOKS

Guidebooks provide valuable insights on steelhead waters and can be very useful aids in planning a trip to unfamiliar waters. Naturally, guidebooks tend to become outdated rather quickly with regard to specific details listed in them, so always double-check fishing regulations and seasons with state fish and game agencies. I have found the following books to be some of the many useful trip-planning guides.

British Columbia

Brown, Rob, *Steelhead River Journal: Skeena*, Portland, OR: Frank Amato Publications, 1997.

Cameron, Neil, et al, *The Essential Guide to Fly Fishing British Columbia*, Calgary, Alberta: Johnson Gorman Publishers, 2003.

Fennelly, John, *Steelhead Paradise*, Portland, OR: Frank Amato Publications, 1989.

Lingren, Art, *Steelhead River Journal: Dean*, Portland, OR: Frank Amato Publications, 2000.

Lingren, Art, *Steelhead River Journal: Thompson*, Portland, OR: Frank Amato Publications, 1994.

Washington

Hogan, Dec, *Steelhead River Journal: Skagit–Sauk*, Portland, OR: Frank Amato Publications, 1996.

Probasco, Steve, *Steelhead River Journal: Hoh*, Portland, OR: Frank Amato Publications, 1999.

Shewey, John, *Washington Blue-Ribbon Fly Fishing Guide*, Portland, OR: Frank Amato Publications, 2003.

Thomas, Greg, *Fly Fisher's Guide to Washington*, Belgrade, MT: Wilderness Adventures Press, 1999.

Oregon

Bachman, Mark, *Steelhead River Journal: Sandy*, Portland, OR: Frank Amato Publications, 1997.

Sheehan, Madelynne Diness, *Fishing In Oregon, Ninth Edition*, Scappoose, OR: Flying Pencil Publications, 2003.

Shewey, John, *On the Fly Guide to the Northwest*, Belgrade, MT: Wilderness Adventures Press, 2002.

Shewey, John, *Oregon Blue-Ribbon Fly Fishing Guide*, Portland, OR: Frank Amato Publications, 1999.

Shewey, John, *Steelhead River Journal: North Umpqua*, Portland, OR: Frank Amato Publications, 1996.

California

Burdick, George, *California's Smith River*, Portland, OR: Frank Amato Publications, 1993.

Freeman, Jim, *California Steelhead*, San Francisco: Chronicle Books, 1984.

Norman, Seth, *Flyfisher's Guide to Northern California*, Belgrade, MT: Wilderness Adventures Press, 2003.

Idaho

Barker, Rocky and Retallic, Ken, *Flyfisher's Guide to Idaho*, Belgrade, MT: Wilderness Adventures Press, 2003.

Shewey, John, *Idaho Blue Ribbon Fly Fishing Guide*, Portland, OR: Frank Amato Publications, 1999.

INDEX